# The Activity of Politics
## and Related Essays

# The Activity of Politics
## and Related Essays

*Wendell John Coats, Jr.*

Selinsgrove: Susquehanna University Press
London and Toronto: Associated University Presses

'0002 63854

Associated University Presses
440 Forsgate Drive
Cranbury, NJ 08512

Associated University Presses
25 Sicilian Avenue
London WC1A 2QH, England

Associated University Presses
P.O. Box 488, Port Credit
Mississauga, Ontario
Canada L5G 4M2

The paper used in this publication meets the requirements
of the American National Standard for Permanence of Paper
for Printed Library Materials Z39.48-1984.

**Library of Congress Cataloging-in-Publication Data**

Coats. Wendell John.
    The activity of politics and related essays / Wendell John Coats,
Jr.
    p.   cm.
Includes bibliographies and index.
    ISBN 0-941664-95-3 (alk. paper)
    1. Political science.   2. Liberalism.   3. Crisis management.
I. Title.
JA71.C55   1989
320—dc19                                                     88-42861
                                                                   CIP

*For Lee and Mary Jane*

# Contents

# Preface: Politics and Moderation

The essays that go together to make up this book were written on different occasions over the past five years and may appear from their titles to have little in common. Their concerns range across the artificial compartments of academic political science to address questions of philosophy, ideology, foreign policy, arms control, educational policy, and so on. Yet the essays were all animated by a few simple ideas about the characteristics of politics, and all owe their shape to my attempts to show how acceptance or rejection of these ideas makes politics wax or wane.

If these few ideas can be compressed into a single sentence, it might be this: That there is a civilized achievement of the West called politics; that it amounts to "the moderate solution to living together";[1] that it is not an illusion or disguise for something else; and that the alternatives to it are all less moderate. In another age, with different insights and blindnesses, exercises such as these essays to define the characteristics of politics might be considered superfluous or even banal. (*Autres temps, autres folies.*) But the challenges to sane living in each age concentrate the mind in particular ways, enhancing our consciousness about certain aspects of what we are doing that have become obscure (or, perhaps have never been brought to light).

The understanding of politics presented in these pages might be summarily described as that part of the thought of Aristotle on politics, and Cicero on the rule of law, that modern liberalism can preserve without hopelessly contradicting itself. Such a synthesis of ideas and practices, providing for individual self-expression within a political framework built of Greek logic and European civility, I refer to by the expression, "politics as the moderate solution to living together." The challenges to this way of living come from extremism of any sort—militarism, pacifism, irrationalism, rationalism. But it is the particular forms of these extremisms in our times—refracted through the medium of modern myopic self-consciousness—that I have tried to identify and analyze. All of those that I discuss are some variant of the combination of extreme democracy and "scientific" control—for example, Marxism, Deweyism, and what I call the arms control–crisis management paradigm for national security. A large amount of space is devoted to analysis of the crisis management paradigm because, in my view, it is the most subtle and least perceived threat to the politics of a republic.

The first essay, "The Activity of Politics," has served for several years as the concluding lecture in my introductory course on politics at Connecticut College. It attempts to lay out systematically the characteristics of politics and the conditions necessary for it to occur, including its proper relationship to armed force. The second essay, "Errors of Marxism," served as the concluding lecture in a semester-long course at Kenyon College on Marx and his disciples; it attempts to show the hostility of Marxism to both politics and civility. The third essay, "Michael Oakeshott's Critique of Rationalism in Politics," was delivered at an annual conference of the Northeastern Political Science Association; it lays out the views of one of the foremost critics of modern rationalist planning. The fourth essay, "Michael Oakeshott as Liberal Theorist," originally appeared in the *Canadian Journal of Political Science*; in attempting to place Oakeshott in the history of political thought, the essay makes a philosophic defense for the particular combination of Aristotelian, Roman, and modern liberal ideas that underlie the account of politics exposited in the first essay of this book. The fifth essay, "The Ideology of Arms Control," originally appeared in the *Journal of Contemporary Studies* in 1982; it presents a view of the arms control–crisis management paradigm as an extreme form of rationalism that attempts unsatisfactorily to substitute technical for political and military solutions. It was reprinted in 1984 by A. L. Chickering in his *Readings in Public Policy*. The six, seventh, and eighth essays were the fruits of a year-long grant in 1983 from the Institute for Educational Affairs to pursue the conclusions of the previous article. They give a more detailed account of the crisis management paradigm and suggest its possible dangers for republican government and political liberty; some of the factual information in these essays is now a bit outdated, but not sufficiently to invalidate the general conclusions. The ninth essay, "The Democratic Self against Moral Individualism," surveys the educational theories of John Dewey in order to show how they fit into and complement the hostility to liberal politics implicit in the tendency of both extreme democracy and modern science to "externalize" or make public *all* standards of decision making, especially in the nuclear age. The tenth essay, "Liberal Democracy and the Time Stream," was prompted by a provocative article of the Italian writer Alberto Moravia;[2] my own essay tries to show that not all of modern liberalism is time bound or "bourgeois," and extends the analysis to consider the political and military dangers of allowing ourselves to become completely immersed in time-bound valuations. The epilogue, "Logic and Civility as 'Will to Power,' " was written expressly for this collection; it tries to show that while politics within the context of logic and civility may not be ethically "neutral," as some have claimed, it still affords the most manageable toleration of diversity available to us.

I shall mention briefly the debts of which I am most conscious. The influence of the ideas of political theorists Michael Oakeshott, Leo Strauss, and Eric Voegelin (introduced to me by Professors Timothy Fuller, Pamela Jensen, and Horst Mewes) looms large in these essays, albeit disguised in a rather Stoic manner of exposition. From Oakeshott's works I learned how to read Hegel and Hobbes, and from those of Strauss and Voegelin, I learned how to read Plato. From my father, Major-General Wendell Coats, I learned to address the relationship of politics to armed force,[3] and to be attentive to the dangers in the overextended application of the crisis management models he first encountered at the Harvard Center for International Affairs, and later in Mr. McNamara's Pentagon. Thanks are owed to Professor Ed Cranz, who helped me to understand better the passage of Aristotle's *Politics* through the middle ages and on into modern liberalism; to the late Professor Bob Horwitz for first-hand lessons in the efficacy of sustained political willpower; to Phil Marcus, Ken Jensen, and the Institute for Educational Affairs for a grant to study the political effects of the arms control–crisis management paradigm; to Professor Paul Seabury and Robert Tucker for their willingness to read my findings in draft, and to Dr. Tom Blau for comment and counsel; to Professor Oakeshott for the kindness of his personal reactions to the *Canadian Journal* article; to Mr. David Wiley of Susquehanna University Press, and the various editors of Associated University Presses, for their interest and help in bringing this collection to publication; and to my colleagues in the Department of Government at Connecticut College for their continuous support in my trials and endeavors. Finally, my own experience as army officer, legislative assistant,[4] and political theory professor has provided me with a unique vantage point from which to assess the contemporary threats to civility and moderation.

## Notes

1. This expression belongs to Leo Strauss, who would surely have objected to some of the uses that I have made of it.

2. Alberto Moravia, "The Terrorist Aesthetic," *Harpers Magazine*, June 1987, 37–44.

3. See Wendell J. Coats, *Armed Force as Power* (New York: Exposition Press, 1966); and idem, "Clausewitz's Theory of War: An Alternative View," *Comparative Strategy* 5, no. 4 (1986): 351–73. (The views in these writings on the relationship of politics to force are more Weberian than are my own.)

4. I worked in 1979 for a young technocrat named Dave Stockman, whose attitudes quickly confirmed for me the accuracy of Oakeshott's observation that the "rationalist" mind is hostile to anything so immersed in chance and contingency as politics.

# The Activity of Politics
## and Related Essays

# 1
# The Activity of Politics

The activity of politics finds itself under attack from diverse quarters these days. The underlying assumption, spoken or not, in all these attacks is the idea that politics be abolished as the basis for human cooperation. These attacks begin in an Augustinian account of government as a punishment for prideful human nature and end in a Marxian and scientific promise of technological redemption, but there is still much other skepticism expressed during the long period they embrace. America, founded by preachers, adventurers, and others on the peripheries of European society, has always found it difficult to accept the necessity of politics for moderate life, *if this idea is made explicit.* "If only each of us would simply do his or her job, there might be no need for politics and politicians," many Americans sigh, and their leaders echo them. And the technocrats stand ready in the wings to second the sentiment.

In what follows, I try to demonstrate that politics is a real activity necessary for moderate life in common, from which there is no more moderate escape. The characteristics of politics I discuss here have their origins in the political practices and reflections of European and American civilization, beginning with Aristotle and ending in modern liberalism. When these characteristics are made explicit in this fashion, I hope that they will hang together logically, and not offend our common sense— *the* political sense. Although in conclusion I shall try for a satisfactory synthesis of the following ideas about politics, I begin by establishing each on its own terms.

The first characteristic of politics, and a defining one, is that it is the activity of attending to the arrangements of the whole society, or the common part of our lives together.[1] I say that politics, or the choice and conduct of policy, involves attending to whole or comprehensive arrangements because it makes decisions about how various other activities—commercial, educational, familial, military, religious, scientific, social, and so on—

are to fit together and receive or be denied resources and legal liberties. Briefly put, politics here is the activity of deciding which other activities wax or wane. If, for example, molecular-cellular-developmental biology is not funded by state legislatures, or is legally restricted by local governments, it is not going to flourish. Or, if capital gains taxes on income from stock sales diminish, stock trading is likely to flourish. Or, if parental prerogatives are circumscribed by law, the importance of the family in education is likely to diminish, and so on.

Furthermore, such decisions take on even more determining influence the longer they stay in place, and the more generations they affect. This is one reason why the politics of a founding, or constitution building, has been viewed as a grander kind of politics—because if it endures, the construction sets the general directions and channels within which a civilization or nation will direct its energies. Or, at a minimum, it sets the horizons for its energies, and closes off certain channels or directions, for example, state economic planning or state religion. This is true for succeeding generations even if the initial written constitution is thought of historically as codifying what people are already doing in practice. Who would care to speculate on the general contours of life in North America today (after diverse waves of immigration) *less* the federal and republican features of the Constitution of 1787?

Politics, then in the exact sense, whether of an infrequent founding kind or of a daily kind choosing policies, is concerned with attending to the arrangements of a whole society. (Even local politics is a microcosm of national politics in this sense, less the requirements for external defense.) A further proof and illustration of this fundamental idea is to be found by considering the kinds of individuals who are most successful at political leadership of their countries. Successful national leaders (and leaders of large subordinate entities) seem as a group to possess the *political* ability to make prudent judgments about ordering priorities among various societal activities that at first appear to have no common denominator. Whether these individuals enter public life from the legal profession, the military, the pulpit, or the world of commerce, their political success begins to show itself (other things being equal) in the evolving ability to transcend their starting places. They begin to mature as politicians and statesmen in learning to balance all sorts of diverse and competing claims for resources and attention, in terms of the health of the whole society.

Those in national politics who continue to view the state from their starting place, and treat it and its problems as those of simply a big store, or a big army, or a big church (instead of *all* of these and more), ultimately define their own limits for us when the nature of the problems facing them expands outside of their particular channel of vision. The case of former President Carter presents an interesting illustration of this point. Carter, a former nuclear engineer who also delivered sermons in his local church, seemed to possess both technocratic and spiritual insights, but lacked (and did not appreciably acquire) the political skills and motivations between these polar opposites necessary to govern the country. He could apparently read and assimilate detailed plans and then appeal spiritually to the whole country to support him, but lacked the political will to go to Congress and gain the real and continuing support necessary for achievable programs. In this sense one might say that Carter could grasp the analogy of the state as a big church and a big factory or submarine, but (although a former officer and farmer) lacked insights from the military and commercial professions about building coalitions with both stick and carrot. These observations apply even more aptly to Mr. Carter's foreign policy.

That politics is the activity of attending to the arrangements of a *whole* society leads to the second of its defining characteristics, that it involves relations among *citizens*—that is, formal equals in subscription to *general* laws framed to avoid conditions of injustice. This very compact idea must be unpacked carefully. The central idea is that political association describes a distinct and distinctive way of being associated, and that relations among citizens differ in an important way from relations among, for example, brothers and sisters, employees, lovers, soldiers, comrades, union members, role performers, ants, beavers. Also implied is that relations between political leaders are in an important way different from relations between employers and employees, parents and children, teachers and students, commanders and soldiers, shop stewards and laborers, queen bees and drones, although there may be aspects of some of these in political relationships.

If political association is a distinctive way of being associated, it must be in acknowledgment of laws sufficiently broad that they specify no specific policies or actions—for example, "to secure the blessings of liberty," or "to provide for the common defense."[2] Anything very specific as the terms of association reduces citizens to mere role performers who do not require a political vocabulary to describe what they are doing, and who risk equating justice with their particular interest. Daily politics, then, arises among equal subscribers in a distinctive realm of freedom existing in the gap between *general* laws and what they must mean when applied in *specific* situations. Does providing for the common defense mean conscription or not? Does providing for the general welfare mean food stamps or not? These answers are worked out in the activity of politics among citizens and leaders subscribing to the same general ideas, but starting from different places and with different opinions about what they must mean in policy today. Nor are such general laws and ideas meaningless in practice as a basis for the general shape of the political order. We may, for example, differ about the meaning of "cruel and unusual punishments," but what might our country look like today without their formal prohibition in the initial bill of rights?

Mundane politics, then, involves working out the meanings of general laws, like those of our Constitution, in the face of a stream of contingencies. As we can observe, this process involves judgment, deliberation, persuasion, compromise, and, sometimes, coercion or its deterrent threat. It is here that we can begin to distinguish political relationships from those among the other kinds of "associates" we have just named. The requirement to grasp general laws and work out their contingent meanings in action and policy through judgment, deliberation and persuasion will distinguish us from lower-order, "gregarious" animals and insects like beavers and ants, which lack this contingent realm of freedom arising in the act of judgment. But what of the other forms of "association" we named? The distinguishing feature here about political association is that the other relationships all arise in the accomplishment of a *substantial* purpose—parents and teachers to form character and impart specific knowledge in the young; employers and employees to produce some product or service; lovers to "lose" themselves in one another; commanders and soldiers to win battles; churches to save souls. However, the purpose of political association, or the "state" as we say now, seems on relection to be simply perpetuation of itself as the self-perpetuating association, or in different words, continuing recognition of itself as a just and legitimate system of authority.

This general purpose may at different times require citizens to win victories, form the character of the young, care for one another, and so on, but none of these aims exhausts the state's purpose, which is highly formal. The state aims to perpetuate recognition of itself and its general laws as the terms of agreement among *citizens*, that is, formal equals in acknowledgment of a system of authority that provides the context for their various substantial purposes. Politics, then, involves substantial actions and policies, such as restraining orders and the military draft, but ones enacted in subscription to more general laws, such as providing for "due process" and the common defense, and carried out as a part of *governance*.

A third essential aspect of politics we have now mentioned in the preceding discussion: politics involves the activities of judgment, persuasion, compromise, and sometimes coercion or its threat. Judgment, or the intellectual act of bridging from a general principle to a particular instance of it, is necessary because the terms of political association are, by definition, general. Persuasion and compromise are necessary to move from individual judgments to cooperative action, because everyone's judgments about the meaning of general laws and what is fair and proper policy will not be the same. (Notice that this problem diminishes as the terms of association become more specific—persuasion and compromise, for example, are not usually thought of as inherent characteristics of military and scientific relationships.) And institutions for coercion are necessary in the event of external threat or when collective legal decisions are ignored. The means of politics, then, are moderate or "politic," relying on persuasion and rational appeal to reconcile differences before resorting to coercive measures. If politics relies only on persuasive measures, then it begins to mutate into religion or philosophy; if only on coercive measures, then it becomes more like military life.

The fourth idea about politics derives from the requirement for persuasion and compromise. It is that rhetoric, in its true sense as the art of persuasive utterance, is a necessary part of the activity of politics. If there is going to be reconciliation of differences among people, then they must listen to one another's points of view. And human beings being what they are, it is often necessary to devote time and thought to getting one's point across. Without delving into past scholastic works of rhetoric, and without being hypocritical, our common sense will direct our attention to several points here. For example, there are times, seasons, and moods when it is better to say some things than others, especially if the matter at hand is not critical.[3] In addition, even when it is the right time to say something, there are still considerations of style, and the amount of detail to be discussed in public. The point obviously is to find the right combination. A serious message may demand a lighter style, for example, to hold an audience's attention. Yet a discussion of rhetoric involves more than points of style. There is the whole issue of metaphor.

Because politics involves communication among persons of diverse interest, background, and specialization, it requires an appropriate metaphorical language that most can understand and will take seriously ("metaphorical" because that is the only way to avoid making major points in a technical language that may exclude parts of the audience). The pragmatic disposition of Americans, for example, makes them ill-disposed to philosophic imagery, but they are more receptive to metaphor with a scientific, technical, or legalistic "ring" to them. Take the general idea that life involves certain risks that can not be prudently eliminated. This thought would not get very far with most American voters in the philosophic form—"chance is an inherent characteristic of the human condition"—but it might get a hearing if expressed as the economic equation that "the price of absolute safety is infinite cost." Similarly, words of scientific imagery like "parameters" and "factors," with the sound of crisp and efficient energy, seem to have an almost magical ability to make Americans feel they are listening to a serious discussion. If, in fact, the matter *is* serious or critical, there is perhaps no harm in using such words to alert them to the situation.[4]

Rhetoric is an indispensable component of especially democratic politics because most people will "know" a political leader only in the realm of appearances, at a distance and with infrequent exposure. This situation has become more or less acute in the age of modern communications depending on one's point of view (does television bring a candidate closer or not?), but it has always existed, even in open-air amphitheaters. This does not mean that politics is *all* appearance or *all* rhetoric (as Socrates' sophist opponents asserted). It does mean, however, that democratic politics among large numbers of people involves a considerable amount of decision in terms of appearances and what they reveal, owing primarily to constraints of time and space.

Yet, as long as this situation is understood and allowed for, it is workable. (Our founders tried to control this problem through federalism, a system permitting serious local or "close-up" governance.) And it is here that rhetoric or the art of persuasion becomes so important for communication under constraints of long distances and limited time. To say in this context that rhetoric is an indispensable part of the political art is to say that leaders are obligated to be very careful and consistent about the signs and symbols they use, because these are what most people must rely on to make judgments about them and their policies. Once the apocryphal story got round, for example, that Franklin Roosevelt loved the song "Home on the Range," it would have been an irrelevant confusion of the public and private realms for him to have proclaimed his distaste for it when it was played to honor him. (And who would have believed him?) As we shall see, this requirement for consistency in mass settings contributes to the occurrence of partisanship in politics, as well.

A fifth idea about politics actually concerns the conditions or context within which it can occur and continue. In addition to a fairly diverse population with differences to reconcile and the leisure to reconcile them, politics also requires a certain relationship to armed force. I have suggested, and common sense confirms, that politics involves both persuasion and coercion (or its potential), even when the authority of leaders to rule is recognized as legitimate, or deriving from agreed-upon procedures. How are the military and police use of armed force related to public order and the occurrence of politics?

The idea of politics, thus far, has been that of an activity of moderately reconciling our differences about policy under freedom of general laws that constitute the terms of political and civil association. More briefly, we might call politics the moderate or civil solution to living together. In this sense, politics as a distinct way of achieving public order and cohesion seems to be a historical achievement of middle and commercial classes and societies—those sufficiently independent to value living in a realm of public freedom, but sufficiently dependent on one another for getting things done to require public means of cooperation and reconciliation. (The very rich have had little need for politics; the very poor little leisure for it; and military and priestly societies little taste for it.)

Part of this moderation, however, has involved a moderate relationship to the use of armed force. This has meant historically sufficient familiarity and skill in its use to *defend* the realm of civil and political freedom from both internal and external aggressors who would substitute less moderate ways of living together for politics. The Greek city-states, for example, where politics began to evolve as a distinct human activity, arose as viable entities coeval with the development of infantry tactics like the phalanx, which allowed successful defense by non-professional or citizen-soldiers against aristocratic cavalry attacks.[5] And the American founders were explicit that the use of armed force would be decided and measured in terms of the requirements of the common *defense*.[6]

Stated in terms of the general relationship between internal or punitive use of force, and external or defensive use of force, moderate political life seems to require that a society tame itself sufficiently so that it preserves public order within its borders, but not so much that it loses the skills and willingness to defend itself against external threats of dominion. Nor need these skills become a full-time occupation for everyone (another danger to politics). The fact that armies composed in part of citizen-soldiers have been capable of successfully defending their countries against military societies in some notable cases suggests a natural advantage in defense over attack.[7] This natural advantage has provided the "slack" in energy and attention necessary for moderate political life to arise and perpetuate itself in other arts and sciences (some with military applications, thus providing even more "slack").

The sixth idea about politics is that it has certain limits that make it incapable of eliminating the human characteristics that helped it to evolve as a recognizable activity in the first place. Whether these limits are observed externally in the history of political societies and the problems they faced, or introspectively in the human psyche, they are present in human affairs and can be reconstructed from the characteristics of politics we have enumerated here. This is not to say that politics cannot be eliminated as the basis for cooperation and order in societies. On the contrary, the actual existence of politics is as historically rare an occurrence as have been middle classes with longevity. Political rule can be prevented or displaced by the command of military dictators, or the management of "enlightened" administrators, or the paternalism of priestly theocrats, and the corresponding displacement of *citizens* under general laws, by soldiers or comrades, role performers in a common enterprise, or "brothers and sisters." Nor need such developments be acknowledged to occur—how many armies, economies, and churches do we see disguised in today's world under the rubric of political associations or states?

Whereas political association can be prevented or abolished, however, it (and the technology it fosters) cannot abolish itself in a "higher" freedom overcoming life's major "dualisms," as the

Marxists and others have claimed. This is simply not possible as long as human beings remain beings who can think *general* thoughts but do only *particular* acts. We cannot "do" generalities like equality in single acts or policies, no matter what the state of technology or the degree of public consensus. Until the end of time, or at least until the evolution of major telepathic powers or the discovery of a drug capable of a state of *sustained* illusion, politics will remain necessary to bridge the gap between political ideals and actions for a society as a whole, unless, of course, a society chooses or accepts in lieu of political rule a form of management—military, corporate, ideological, scientific—that assigns or inculcates specific tasks or roles as the *primary* basis for general order, rather than simply the basis for administration and law enforcement.

Before trying to pull together this cluster of defining ideas about politics, two related ideas must be addressed briefly. One is the relationship to politics of partisanship and parties; the other, the relationship to politics of governance and government.

Is partisanship essential to politics as we have defined it here? The answer lies I believe in the nature of political action involving large numbers of people, and will take us back over some ground covered in the discussion of rhetoric. Partisanship—if not to a formal party, then to certain sets or kinds of ideas—appears to be necessary in large-scale popular politics because of the time and energy required to overcome inertia to get things accomplished, and the importance of consistency in the symbols conveyed in mass, political communication: Possibly, in small republics or in local politics, it is feasible for conscientious and independent citizens and leaders to evaluate anew each issue, but in modern, democratic politics these judgments have to be extended to programs as a whole, if something is to be accomplished in a term of office. After all, politics does occur in a realm of action where competition arises not merely between ideas, but directly between the bearers or partisans of those ideas. When the time becomes right for a set of ideas, we make their bearers our governors or "steerers." (And there is still a place in the *center* of all this for "independents" as the balancers of partisan claims.)

Government, then, beyond the obvious need for specific administrative performances, arises in the requirement for a steerer or conductor of policy through the stream of contingencies facing the body politic at any moment. To restate this last relationship, we might say that politics in the broad sense breaks down into the activities of persuasion and choice about platform or program (politics narrowly), *and* the conduct of policy (governance). In times and places where we see *only* administration and governance, to the exclusion of persuasion and compromise in the choice of policy, we do not think of "politic" behavior as occurring. We can also observe that rotation of partisan governors teaches "politic" behavior, that is, behavior conducive to the moderate reconciliation of differences about policy.

Let us try to gather up this cluster of characteristics, and see if they elucidate political activity sufficiently to repay the effort of this defining exploration. The picture of politics sketched here is that of an activity which moderately reconciles differences about policy among citizens, or formal equals under the freedom of general laws acknowledged to have legitimacy. It involves judgment, artful persuasion, compromise, coercion, partisanship, and governance. Finally, although it may be abolished by something less free, politics is incapable of eliminating itself (as a basis for living together) in some "higher" freedom that transcends the fundamental "dualisms of existence." Politics, then, as a distinct human activity, has been viewed as the moderate or civil solution to living together, and as a historic achievement of the middle or moderate classes, although we may certainly hope that it can be passed on to others.

To compress a way of living into explicit and condensed formulations is usually a sign that it is under attack or in a process of deformation. We gather up the characteristics of what we are doing in compact abbreviations to define them and protect them from loss, the way we might gather up our belongings when thieves or despoilers come. And that is just what I have been doing in this exercise of definition—trying to gather up the characteristics and postulates of politics in the face of a series of overt, covert, inadvertent, and purposeful attacks upon it in our times. Perhaps through such exercises we can become clearer about what politics does for us in creating a realm of public freedom between the poles of general laws and specific policies; and how its various characteristics have evolved and cohere in making civility and moderation possible. With these insights in at least the backs of their minds, the partisans of politics may be slightly more on guard against those who, in the name of whatever cause or interest, would substitute the specific tasks and warm certainties of comrades, role performers, or fellow therapists and patients, for the spirited independence of citizens.

1984

# Notes

1. Even a society like our own, in which the scope of explicit governance is limited, could acknowledge the initial decision to limit government in certain areas to be a *political* decision, and one perpetuated by subsequent political decisions codified in laws.

2. "Political association," then, may be seen to differ in our modern liberal usage from that of the ancient Greeks whose expression it was. For them, "political association" described a closer and more substantial relationship concerned to habituate citizens to a certain *ethos*. (See, for example, book 3 of Aristotle's *Politics*.) The interesting question here is whether the ancient Greeks achieved a separation of politics from education and character formation.

3. On the other hand, there are times when circumstances become so critical that uncorrupt political leadership must go against this canon of rhetoric in order to maintain the body politic and say things people may not wish to hear. Political leadership, for example, may find it necessary in times of justified fear to fortify a people's spirits; or, in times of unjustified anger, to dampen their spirits. Even here, however, there will still be present considerations of rhetoric, or artful persuasion.

4. However, there might be some long-range dangers for the activity of politics if the *only* sources of metaphor were to become those of science and technology.

5. See, for example, J. B. Bury, ed., *The Cambridge Ancient History* (Cambridge: Cambridge University Press, 1927), 6:695–96.

6. See, for example, *The Federalist*, nos. 23 and 41.

7. See, for example, Carl von Clausewitz, *On War*, eds. Michael Howard and Peter Paret (Princeton: Princeton University Press, 1976), book 6 ("Defense").

# 2
# Errors of Marxism

This essay is the outcome of a commonsensical rereading of the basic works of Marx and Engels. It aims throughout to achieve a consistent reflection of Marxism, in the mirror of common sense, understood as a kind of political sense, concerned with balancing competing and dissimilar priorities and needs, in the context of the fundamental structure of reality. Thus, it is always suspicious of claims to overcome the need for its balancing function through alleged elimination of one or more of the fundamental tensions of human existence.

The heart of Marx's political theory is that the fundamental tensions between individual and community that have characterized all political life heretofore can be finally overcome in the culmination of an economically driven, historical process of fluid contraries, helped along by Marx and his followers, contemporary and posthumous.[1] In especially the early writings, we are presented with a vision of a final, communist society in which individuals grasp their true essence as "species-beings"; in which economic scarcity has been eliminated following the collapse, appropriation, and collectivization of highly productive capitalist systems of technology; in which the state and politics have withered away to a minimal administrative apparatus; and in which all "labor" freely and playfully for themselves, now as shepherds, now painters, now book critics, and so on, without specializing, without being fitted into a division of labor.[2]

Under pure communism, we are told, man will have returned to himself as a social, that is, cooperatively laborious, being, but this time without the natural and artificial necessities requiring involuntary labor. Society's resources will apparently be directed toward correcting nature's inequal dispensations of talent and energy by providing for each according to his needs, in a most comprehensive sense; and apparently, through a decrease in exigency, by equalizing the relative importance of all human activities from pottery to philosophy.[3]

The reputed advantages of the new community over the old liberal state and society include the elimination of the various compartments of civilization, which allegedly alienate men from themselves and from the products of their labor. No longer will we have an abstract, political realm of formal rights; no longer a private, egoistic realm of acquisition and diverse activity and association; and no longer a religious realm for expressing deference to a transcendent power other than man's own creative ability to transform his future through his own labor.[4] In brief, we are to expect a new, vague kind of putative "oneness" arising among comrades cultivating their now politically inconsequential diversities without impinging on one another's prerogatives to do likewise—and all of this made possible through the unification of economic life, and without the various constitutional devices heretofore necessary to create a realm of civil freedom in the common part of our lives together.

However, as we never cease hearing, there is involved here as well an even grander and more mysterious unity—the so-called unity of theory and practice, of philosophy and political action. Both the motor that drives the historical process and the map it follows and charts are to be strangely united, such that neither exactly guides the other (although political action and revolution remain of great importance.) The truth of theoretical speculation can now be known only pragmatically—that is, in action—and action has come to mean a political program whose general guidelines have been prescribed by Marx and Engels based upon their reading of the direction of an economically and dialectically driven, world-historical process.[5]

Finally, in the later writings, as part of a demonstration of the mechanics and inevitability of this historical process, we are given an economic tour de force, a sort of "Phenomenology of Labor." In *Capital* and elsewhere, Marx attempts to follow the various mutations of the "only" value-creating force, human labor,[6] in order to demonstrate that capitalism must eventually collapse as it continues to displace human labor with technology, because the latter is allegedly incapable of providing the economic slack of the former, which can be "exploited." Capitalist technology thus provides no escape valve, on this view, for the expanding revolutionary energy of the human exhaust cast off by capitalism's growing concentration of ownership and automation of production.[7]

As has often been noted, the appeal of Marx's complete vision reaches into both rational and irrational experience. In addition to a simple "scientific" and mechanical theory of Western history, polity, and economy, providing instant "education" for those without the opportunity to acquire a real one, the Marxist vision also produces an appeal to the irrational and religious side of man. It promises in the "here and now" (or, at least, the "here and then") something that religion generally promises in another time and place—the overcoming of contradictions and major tensions (and with them the need for politics), the time of everlasting peace.

Critically consider first the "scientific" side of the theory. There are many problems with its philosophic, political, historical, psychological, and economic reductionisms that deny common sense and insight about the fundamental structure of reality and its tensions. The critique that follows attempts to represent the unflinching and unoriginal voice of common sense against the gamut of fantastic Marxist claims. The very fact that such obvious points require to be made so explicitly is dismal testimony to the headway that these inversions of reality are making in our unsettled times.

1. The attempt to collapse theory and practice, philosophy and political action, into a single realm of experience denies the fundamental structure of reality—that whereas *thought* can be either universal or particular in scope, *action* is always particular.[8] (Try to think of a *general* action except perhaps one of explosive destruction.) There is simply no way to bridge *from* particular actions, such as feeding the poor, *to* general ideas, such as equality, except in acts of judgment and deliberation. For society as a whole the activity that bridges these two realms by way of procedures and prudence is the activity of politics. Hence, Marx's claim that by collapsing the distinction between *Theoria* and *Praxis*, he can also eliminate politics as the activity that bridges them, is simple non-sense, albeit abstractly stated. As long as human beings remain beings constituted in the duality of thought and action (in spite of fleeting escapes), and beings inclined to associate in terms of general ideas such as achieving justice, then the activity of politics (deliberation and compromise about achieving general aims), with all of its impermanent and fuzzy outcomes, will remain with us.

Although it may be possible to live primarily in a realm of thought, or primarily in a realm of action, or consciously to embody the tension between the two, the misguided attempt to collapse the two such that citizens come to believe they can "do" generalities can only mean a horrible reduction in awareness that forgets what it once knew. Lenin's criticism of his "infantile" leftist opponents is equally applicable to both Marx and Lenin: "it is a glaring theoretical error to apply the yardstick of world history to practical politics."[9] How else shall we judge men whose "political" program is to "abolish philosophy by realizing it"?

2. Ignoring the inherent gap between general ideas and particular action leads to the denigration of theory and careful thinking, and over time, to the weakening of the rational part of the personality through disuse. This, in turn, leads to fuzziness in public discussion about which things theoretical intellect can genuinely contribute to practical life—for example, critical ideas that could demonstrate beforehand grand mistakes better not committed. That is, philosophy may not be able to tell us expressly what to do in particular situations, but sometimes it can tell us what *not* to do[10]—for example, attempt to eliminate the gap between general thought and particular action (outside of the realm of art and poetry where it is a proper aim).

This error also breeds utopian confusion about what can actually be accomplished in political action, the summit of which may not proceed beyond providing a general equality of opportunity for diverse talents, certainly not the capability to make all into philosophers (if we could even remember what philosophy was once it had been transformed into a guidepost solely for practical action).

3. The Marxian theory of history with its simple and schematized epochs (feudalism, capitalism) and categories (substructure, superstructure) is anything but a theory of the *history* of human actions, aspirations, and ideas made intelligible in the light of people's own understandings or misunderstandings. Marxian "history" is plain and simple a past plenitude of experience tortuously squeezed into the reductivist channels of "dialectical materialism." This is a possible kind of explanation, and a very simple one at that, but whatever else, it is not *history,* a detailed story of human beings responding to their circumstances as they understood or misunderstood them.[11]

4. Marxian claims of *ultimate* economic determinism in any epoch are either banal, suggesting no more than that there will be some consistency in the economic, political, religious, and cultural ideas and institutions of a civilization; or these claims are simply false, especially in the case of modern capitalism and modern science, whose complicated religious and political ori-

gins were never seriously investigated by either Marx or Engels. (Could, for example, modern science ever have developed without the propagation for a millennium and a half by Christianity of a cosmology of beginnings rather than ends?)[12]

5. Marx's well-known "theory of ideology"—that consciousness is determined by material conditions and all thought is the articulation of a life interest, awares or unawares—is equally applicable to Marx's own thought, and to this very idea. That this criticism has been made many times makes it no less true, nor lessens the urgency to continue to assert it against Marx. In times of grand popular illusions and inversions, one of the legitimate functions of scholarship is surely to state what was once the obvious. If Marx's charge is allowed to stand even by implication, then rational argument for most people is denigrated to a political tactic, exclusively, and their latent, cynical suspicions about the uses of intellect falsely confirmed.

6. Marx's economic analysis of capitalism, even on Marx's own terms, is highly one-sided, refusing to concede that owners and managers of enterprises also expend some of their "vital energy" in the productive process, that is, that they creatively contribute to value. Clearly they do, as mortality statistics indicate, and thus the idea of one-sided exploitation is simply false. In addition, Marx's expectations about the consequences of advanced technology are both *overestimated* and *underestimated*, the former in regard to their ability to liberate human potential from the need for political controls. Elimination of scarcity, even if it could be done, would not eliminate the desire of some individuals to have more of the same, or the desire of a smaller number of individuals to dominate the others, solely for the sake of domination.[13] On the other hand, Marx underestimates the ability of capitalist technology to create new jobs and economic opportunities faster than they eliminate old ones, as the evidence of the past century shows. Nor can capitalism's success in bettering the economic conditions of its peoples be explained exclusively as the result of its unfair exploitation of the rest of the world. To exploit, in Marxist terms, means to create nothing of value oneself, and that is a patently absurd charge in this case.[14]

7. As a consequence of the combination of reductivist analyses, and pseudophilosophic intimations that the truth of communism can be known only when it is achieved, there is lacking in Marx's writings a sustained political analysis of the tensions between the individual and the community. (There is nothing here along the lines of even a Rousseau, who, for example,

explored in some detail the possibilities of overcoming the major tensions of politics on a broad scale through an education to make nonphilosophic but morally autonomous citizens.) Hence, there is lacking a serious exploration by Marx or Engels of which political tensions advanced technology might be able to alleviate, and which ones will be likely to abide with us—for example, tensions between citizens and institutions of authority, between individualist and collectivist personalities, or between potentially tyrannical factions, even in conditions of technological plenty, if communism were capable of achieving that.

Yet, as experience has shown, reciting a litany of the analytic deficiencies in Marxist theory will not suffice to dissuade many people from continuing to embrace it, or at least remain silently sympathetic toward its ultimate goals. Perhaps for few people can the demonstrations of logic refute the hopes of fantastic visions, especially when they are already convinced that intellectual conclusions are merely and always the articulation of some's "life interest." Yet there may be a kind of practical or emotional refutation of Marxism in the visionary realm, if we can tarnish the image of future communism. And we might do this *not* by more critical speculation about its problematic aspects, given human nature and its vainglorious and domineering instincts, but by holding up a brighter image for inspection, the image of our own liberal civilization in the mirror of the present.

Marx's central criticism of liberal civilization in "On the Jewish Question," and elsewhere, is that its fragmentation of life into various and distinct compartments—political, religious, economic, social—is some sort of grand hypocrisy that results in frustration, alienation, psychic disharmony, and so on. (To be preferred, Marx tells us, is a new kind of species unity, achievable not in another life, but here in future communism.) Yet, the contours and fissures of modern liberal civilization may be seen in a much different light—as an ingenious achievement, a myriad of diverse realms of activity and experience, each with its own ways and means; an extraordinary series of opportunities to be relished, nurtured, and enjoyed by those happy enough to acquire the manners, habits, skills, and fortune to find entry into any one or many of them. (Perhaps no one can pass through *all* the doors.) May it not be that it is the preservation of this civilized achievement that still affords the greatest possibilities for human potential in all its depths, aspects, and varieties?

By being initiated into civilization, we do acquire different habits, manners, and skills for life's various compartments—for the dining room, the playing field, the bedroom, the place of worship, the political forum, the dance floor, the various and diverse places of business, the pool hall, the graveside, the maternity room. Yet this is not a source of personal hypocrisy and alienation to be abandoned for some notional and vague sense of unity or species (or "natural self" in Rousseau's version), but a great and fragile achievement that might not have been, and which might not be in the future if we eliminate it because everyone cannot pass through all the doors, all the time. On the contrary, within the realm of the possible, this *is* the realistic possibility Marx is searching for as an alternative to performing a single function, an alternative to the Socratic, "one man, one art." Again, it may be that the peak of the political art is to provide the *general* conditions in which there is fair opportunity for anyone who can acquire the skills and good fortune to pass through any particular door, to be able to do so without formal restriction. This may be one sound idea we can accept from the eighteenth-century European and American theorists of progress—that an extended republic, by incorporating the stability of large regimes and some of the equality of small democracies, reaches the peak of *constitutional* development. All subsequent progress must occur individually, or at least privately, within the realm of civil freedom created by its constitutional authority.

As for a sense of phychic unity beyond that which can be achieved in love, worship, art, philosophy, introspection, and intermittent association with others, it is necessary to face a simple fact. No one, since the advent of Christianity (and its moral elevation of the individual soul) as a civilizational phenomenon, is going to be able to return to the political unity of the small, slave-supported Greek city-state. And the Marxist vision of a *polis* with technology in lieu of slaves, with its reductivist and immoderate consequences for human freedom and self-governance, should be sufficient deterrent to the continued attempt to do so.

1983

## Notes

1. Karl Marx and Friedrich Engels, *Manifesto of the Communist Party*, in *The Marx-Engels Reader*, 2nd ed., ed. Robert C. Tucker (New York: W. W. Norton

and Company, 1978), 473–91. Unless otherwise noted, all works cited hereafter are from the Tucker edition.

2. Karl Marx, *The German Ideology*, part I, section C, 193–200.

3. Ibid.

4. Karl Marx, *On the Jewish Question*, 26–46.

5. Karl Marx, *Contribution to the Critique of Hegel's "Philosophy of Right": Introduction*, 53–65; and *Communist Manifesto*, 483–91; and *Theses on Feuerbach*, 143–45.

6. Karl Marx, *Capital*, 306.

7. For a critical discussion, drawing upon especially the third volume of *Capital*, see Thomas Sowell, *Marxism: Philosophy and Economics* (New York: William Morrow, 1985), 106–42.

8. See, for example, Aristotle, *Nicomachean Ethics*, 2.7.

9. Lenin, *Left-Wing Communism—An Infantile Disorder*, in *The Lenin Anthology*, ed. Robert C. Tucker (New York: W. W. Norton and Company, 1975), 579.

10. See, for example, Michael Oakeshott, *Experience and Its Modes* (Cambridge: Cambridge University Press, 1933), 1–8.

11. For such a view of history, see Oakeshott, *Experience*, 86–168.

12. On the medieval origins of the modern scientific outlook, see Michael Foster, "The Christian Doctrine of Creation and the Rise of Modern Natural Science," *Mind*, 43, no. 172 (October 1934); 446–68.

13. See, in this connection, Aristotle, *Politics*, 2.7.

14. Marx, of course, was tied to this absurdity owing to his mysterious, "philosophic" starting point—that the only "value-creating substance" was something called "homogeneous human labor" (*Capital*, 1,1,1.). This position, in turn, seems to have been a logical necessity to accommodate a more fundamental argument—that *all* consciousness and society were the product of human labor to remake its material conditions. And this starting point seems to have been a tactical position from which to accomplish Marx's life-long goal (if we may believe his graveside eulogy by Engels), the overthrow of capitalism. The first step in that revolution was to assure doubtful revolutionaries that the religion, laws, and social institutions of capitalist and liberal civilization were *all* simply the epiphenomena of a certain set of economic arrangements and, hence, without strong claims to awe, reverence, or longevity.

# Michael Oakeshott's Critique of Rationalism in Politics

Born in 1901, and educated at Cambridge, Michael Oakeshott was for many years Professor at the London School of Economics and Political Science where he taught a seminar in the history of political philosophy that covered the political experiences of ancient Greece, ancient Rome, and medieval and modern Europe. His major works include *Experience and Its Modes* (1933), *Rationalism in Politics* (1959), and *On Human Conduct* (1975).

## Modern Rationalism

Oakeshott uses the expression "modern Rationalism"[1] to refer to a post-Renaissance intellectual tradition first clearly discernible in the thought of Bacon and Descartes, and (without their reservations) characterized by belief in the importance of certain and sovereign techniques of knowledge, capable of being applied by almost anyone to almost any subject matter. Oakeshott distinguishes this rationalism from ancient and medieval rationalism by suggesting that it has combined the worst of the claims for reason of both—broad scope and scholastic rigidity, respectively. He suggests that this approach to knowledge has invaded almost every field of human activity since its distinct appearance in the seventeenth century, and has become progressively more vulgar in each succeeding century, such that what was once "The Art of . . ." has now become "How to . . . in Ten Easy Lessons."

Oakeshott characterizes Rationalism as the belief that all real knowledge is technical knowledge susceptible of formulation in precepts capable of universal application at distinct starting and

This essay was prepared for presentation to the Northeastern Political Science Association, November 1985, Philadelphia, Pennsylvania.

ending points. He contrasts it with his own view that all concrete knowledge and skill is fluid, and consists of both technical knowledge that *can* be put in precepts and books, and practical knowledge of timing and context that is so general and subtle that it can only be acquired in patient practice and apprenticeship. Oakeshott is careful to distinguish Rationalism from modern science and the modern industrial economy, both of which, insofar as they possess real skill, also contain elements of both technical and practical knowledge. (When their insights are put in books, of course, all that is passed on is the technical part of knowledge.)

Oakeshott makes both a philosophic and practical critique of this approach to knowledge. Philosophically, he suggests that Rationalism's claim of certainty and control through distinct beginnings and endings is an illusion, and he cites Pascal's view that in human affairs the probable is more certain than the certain. Oakeshott also suggests that Rationalism has an erroneous view of the human mind in conceiving of a method of reason that can be separated from its historically acquired subject matter. Finally, Oakeshott suggests that Rationalism makes a practical error in thinking that making conduct self-conscious and bringing it before the "bar of reason" is always desirable— usually self-consciousness results in the loss of fluid rhythms that are a necessary component of all skillful practical action. Except in emergencies, when balance is already lost, the proper place of intellect is as critic, not generator, of practical action, and in the lives of both individuals and societies.[2]

In brief, Rationalism mistakes technical knowledge, or knowledge in propositional form, for the whole of knowledge. But precepts, Oakeshott suggests, are simply abbreviations of some previous activity, and remain insoluble until they are submerged in the "acid of practice."

## Rationalism in Politics

Oakeshott suggests that Rationalism's invasion of politics,[3] a realm of diplomacy traditionally grounded in the makeshift, came by way of the combination of political inexperience and political opportunity over the past four centuries, and has been so plausible that for the most part it has covered up to its practitioners their own lack of political education. Not to have a rational plan or doctrine is now considered not be serious—

witness Hayek's *Road to Serfdom*, a plan to resist planning that thus still falls within the Rationalist style of politics.

The combination of political inexperience and the opportunity to engage in politics produces the need for a crib, a shortcut to practical knowledge, contained in the propositions of a book. (Oakeshott suggests that it takes from two to three generations to acquire a profession, including politics.) Oakeshott discusses three well-known European political cribs, constructed to deal with the political inexperience of "the new ruler, of the new ruling class, and of the new political society." Yet if Machiavelli at least offered himself as well as his book to the new prince, and if Locke was at least abbreviating the *historic* habits and rights of Englishmen in the *Second Treatise*, no similar redeeming observation may be said for the abstractions of Marx and Engels. Writing for the largest and most politically inexperienced class of modern Europe, these two were the creators of "the most stupendous of our political rationalisms."

In its political form, Rationalism has become the politics of the felt need interpreted by an ideology and, in its moral form, the self-conscious pursuit of ideals and precepts. Oakeshott's critique of these activities follows from his critique of Rationalism in general. Mistaking its origins for "nature," or "truth," or "reason," rather than the modification of some historically evolved way of living, Rationalism deceives itself into thinking that it can self-conciously and successfully recreate its own political and moral life from new beginnings. Lacking the insight that unselfconscious traditions are flexible with regard to change, it resolves political life into a series or succession of crises and problems to be resolved by yet another tour de force of "unaided" reason. A society under sustained Rationalist direction comes to lose the natural rhythm that exists when intellect retains its proper place as a critic and guardian against superstition and imbalance.[4] (Philosophy, says Oakeshott, cannot tell us what to do in practical life, but it can tell us what *not* to do, tell us when we are being irrelevant.[5]). Additionally, as the traditions of a society become Rationalist themselves, the view of life as a series of problems to be solved becomes even more plausible, though still at the expense of genuine skills.

As alternatives, Oakeshott offers the "pursuit of intimations," or making explicit or legal only what is already being done in practice;[6] he cites the device of "legal fictions" as a traditional way of meeting change; and he is keen on the idea of the authority of law deriving from its relative neutrality with regard to substantial policies. And in his theoretical writing he attempts to sever philosophy, history, and art from all practical considerations. Still, Oakeshott does not seem optimistic about the recovery of political balance for an age in which the Rationalist vocabulary of war and crisis management keeps center stage owing to its own generation of a world situation of almost permanent war and crisis, in the name of "rational" solutions to further crises. Even where new rulers sense the shortcoming of the "book" and fall back on their own experience, it is usually experience acquired in a profession other than politics, and hence not appropriate.

## Critique of Platonic Rationalism

Oakeshott, a benevolent skeptic who "would do better if he only knew how," is obviously dubious of any view that would assign preeminence in human life to bald inquiry and the pursuit of "Truth."[7] He implies that the satisfaction hoped for in such activity could be better sought in poetic or aesthetic contemplation, and without the attendant dangers of the vulgarized search for "Truth" in practical and political existence. Yet Oakeshott has an even more specific critique to make of Platonic discussions of the form or *eidos* of a thing. It is the failure to see the spontaneous and creative character of all experience, and the subsequent attempt to conceive of all human activity as craft or fabrication, which copies an already existing archetype.

On Oakeshott's view, the substantial and formal aspects of experience, *what* is experienced and *how* it is experienced, arise simultaneously or poetically—hence the difficulty of finding distinct beginnings to which to apply a "rational" method." The method and subject matter of all activity arise in a fluid interaction, driven by the "desire" of both the method and the matter, the *how* and *what*, for the unattainable goal of assimilating the other.[8] For Oakeshott, Plato's theoretical articulation of an archetype was in fact a kind of aesthetic contemplation, and Plato mistook the unique character of a poetic or artistic creation (which momentarily unified the duality of the *how* and *what* of experience), for a blueprint to be copied. But for Oakeshott, "there is in fact no way of determining an end for an activity in advance of the activity itself."[9] Hence, in the end, a critique of modern Rationalism for Oakeshott requires tracing back its central error to the peculiar blindness of Greek *Theoria*, the failure to grasp the poetic character of experience.

## Critique of Rationalism and the "Rule of Law"

Oakeshott is known for a "conservative" view of law, which conceives of it as empty as possible of instrumental and substantial purposes.[10] His discussion of civil rather than political association reflects his resistance in theoretical renderings to permitting a link back to the substantial moral and educational purposes of the Greek *politeia* or political association. This view is consistent with, and supported by, Oakeshott's view of experience and practical skill.

If the character of experience and skill is in fact fluid and creative, then there are no distinct beginnings or endings for the abstract intellect to manipulate. Ruling cannot be exclusively a craft or *techne* because the intellect will always be subject somewhat to its own political manipulations after they are multiplied by society; hence, intellect will be a part of a process that partially controls *it*; hence, it will be a part of its own subject matter or, by definition, part of a *creative* act. Failure to recognize this poetic character of all experience will result in loss of skill as intellect attempts an explicit control of things that it is not in the nature of things to permit. The proper role of intellect, again, is as critic, not generator, of practical action. The mind for Oakeshott is not a device for abstract thinking, and the spring of conduct is not a set of premeditated precepts to be applied. Knowing *how* to do something is a complex of evolved habits that constitute the "mind" and contain as well the knowledge of when to act and when not to act in any particular activity; and precepts are simply abbreviations, modified in practice, of what we are already doing.

The societal arrangements that reflect and accommodate this understanding best (because they evolved historically with it) are those that conceive of no *substantial* purpose for a society to accomplish beyond recognition of its general laws as the authoritative context for the achievement of somebody's substantial purposes. Or, to say this more generally, this understanding is best reflected in the manners of civility. Allegiance to the procedures by which lesser laws are made is the best hope for avoiding all sorts of Baconian and visionary political purposes destructive of genuine skill and societal rhythm in their reductionist (i.e., Rationalist) views of human activity.

## Evaluation and Critique

In his early "phenomenology" of experience, and in his later popular essays, Oakeshott has gone some way in bringing to the attention of a civilization beguiled by the image of societal engineering the dangers and limits of such a narrow and reductionist approach to human life and purposes. He has done this by careful demonstration that the form and content, the "how" and "what" of all skillful activity evolve simultaneously and may not be grafted individually onto other activities without a penalty—the penalty paid by societies, for example, that put into political power those trained in abstract management or administration, or in some other field entirely. And, I have argued elsewhere,[11] Oakeshott's late work, On Human Conduct, deserves to establish him as one of the preeminent political theorists of modern individualism. Here, and by way of concluding, I shall simply discuss one relevant point that I think Oakeshott has not gotten quite right.

I have mentioned that in his major theoretical account of modern European political experience, Oakeshott discusses civil association with no extrinsic purpose as a possible form of association implied and on occasion achieved in the European past. Although he discusses "politics" as the activity of attending to the general arrangements of such a society, Oakeshott finds little place for the idea of political association in the experience of the diverse characters who emerged in the breakup of the medieval realms.[12]

Oakeshott's reasoned defense of this position seems to be his view that there is no such thing as a political explanation—that politics is not an explanatory language any more than poetry and can only be explained in the theoretical languages of history or philosophy.[13] If I understand him correctly, I believe that this is not so.

A political explanation, following Aristotle, is one that explains, or makes less opaque and mysterious, an event in terms of the observed tendencies, reoccurrences, and adaptive requirements of a political body or polis. Now, if I follow Oakeshott, he is implying that because we no longer live in small, posttribal polis associations, we can no longer have political explanations, carefully speaking, but only exhortations. Or, perhaps in his strange claim that Aristotle was on his way to attaining the idea of civility,[14] Oakeshott means to imply that political explanation has always been illusory.

In fact, the issue seems to be more complex. Although we are separated from Aristotle by Roman law, Christian and secular self-consciousness, and by the extended size and diversity of our bodies politic, there are clearly observations of Aristotle's political science that still apply, sometimes undiluted, to modern politics. For Oakeshott's claim that there is no political explanation, I would substitute the idea that there in fact is, albeit refracted and reflected through modern self-consciousness of context. Consider, for example, Machiavelli's observation in the *Discourses* that expansive foreign policies are characteristic of republics in which the democrats or "the many" are the guardians of liberty (owing to the expansive appetites of "the many"). If diluted for the development of "soft" modern commerce, this observation still *explains* politically, and might be of some use in projections about policy without specifying any particular policy, the choice and details of which could be worked out in practice.

There are, in brief (and in spite of Oakeshott's denial), certain perennial problems that arise in the unavoidable accommodations made among the various *types* of human beings necessary to generate self-sufficient communities of any size; and to recognize this and begin to observe the recurring patterns and limits of these accommodations is to explain *politically*. What we may learn from Oakeshott here is the insight that such political observations may have only the most tangential connection to the daily problems of rule and governance; nor can the gulf between political explanation and governance be bridged by mere prudence in judgment and action. Different mediations of experience arise in different apprenticeships, and the *most* that any one of them can pass on to any other may be indications of when it is being irrelevant, or overstepping its limits. To see this is to see the possibilities for public moderation (i.e., civility) grounded in appreciation of the problematic character or all human activity rather than in the quest for psychic harmony.

1985

## Notes

1. Unless otherwise noted, all points in this first section are taken from the 1947 essay, "Rationalism in Politics," in Michael Oakeshott, *Rationalism in Politics* (London: Methuen and Co., 1962), 1–36.

2. See, in this connection, Michael Oakeshott, "The Tower of Babel," in *Rationalism in Politics*, 59–79.

3. Unless otherwise noted, all points in this section are taken from the essay "Rationalism in Politics."

4. See Oakeshott, "The Tower of Babel."

5. See Michael Oakeshott, *Experience and Its Modes* (Cambridge: Cambridge University Press, 1933).

6. See Michael Oakeshott, "Political Education," in *Rationalism in Politics*, 111–36.

7. Unless otherwise noted, all points in this section are taken from pages 218–21 of Michael Oakeshott, "The Voice of Poetry in the Conversation of Mankind," in *Rationalism in Politics*.

8. This is the thesis of Oakeshott's 1933 work, *Experience and Its Modes*. The drive of the formal and substantial aspects of experience to extinguish each other is called the unattainable desire for what is "satisfactory in experience." Oakeshott later suggested that the closest approximation to overcoming this tension in experience was to be found in fleeting moments of poetic or aesthetic experience, but certainly not in philosophy. See Oakeshott, "The Voice of Poetry in the Conversation of Mankind."

9. Oakeshott, *Rationalism in Politics*, 91.

10. See Michael Oakeshott, "On Being Conservative," in *Rationalism in Politics*, 168–96; "On the Civil Condition," in *On Human Conduct* (Oxford: Oxford University Press, 1975), 108–84; and "The Rule of Law," in *On History* (Oxford: Basil Blackwell, 1983), 119–64.

11. Wendell J. Coats, Jr., "Michael Oakeshott as Liberal Theorist," *Canadian Journal of Political Science* 18, no. 4 (December 1985): 773–87.

12. See Oakeshott, "On the Civil Condition."

13. Oakeshott, *Rationalism in Politics*, 327.

14. Oakeshott, *On Human Conduct*, 110–11.

# 4

# Michael Oakeshott as Liberal Theorist

My purpose here is not to attempt to categorize the thought of Professor Oakeshott solely for the sake of categorizing. Rather, I hope to show that in his major works Oakeshott has made one of the most interesting and logically coherent statements ever of the liberal point of view, and is to be considered as one of the preeminent political theorists of modern European individualism. If this is the case, then his work requires to be studied for the light it may shed on liberalism as a coherent tradition of political theorizing. At first glance, it may seem mischievous or even mean-spirited to discuss the "liberalism" of Michael Oakeshott. As is well known, he dislikes the hasty and abbreviated approach to politics implicit in "isms" of any sort. Further, he himself uses the word "liberal" in a narrower, historical fashion to designate a view, traceable to John Locke, which started from a position of "natural rights" to argue for the limitation of sovereign authority, and which evolved into claims for material benefits from the state (*"Salus populi, suprema lex!"*).[1]

## 1

Yet, making explicit what is already in the word itself, I believe it is not unfair to use "liberal in the history of political thought to indicate a view of the state as subordinate to, and arising from, the freedom of individual conscience—or sometimes individual appetite—regardless of whether the claim is grounded in some "natural right." (Otherwise, we should have to deny the epithet "liberal" to a writer such as John Stuart Mill, who defended individual liberty not from "nature" but for its effects at a certain historical moment.) And I emphasize the *freedom* of individual

This article first appeared in the *Canadian Journal of Political Science / Revue canadienne de science politique* 18, no. 4 (December 1985): 773–87. Permission to reprint it here is gratefully acknowledged.

conscience to distinguish this view from that of ancient writers like Plato and Aristotle, who saw political association as a means for *habituating* nonphilosophic citizens to moral virtues, regardless of the issue of individual judgment and choice.

From this starting point, the liberal view usually moves to the necessity that obligation to authority arises from the consent of individuals. In some accounts, it conceives of the state as an executed contract, or the result of one, created by the acts of individuals. Emphasis is usually placed upon individual rights delimiting the role of the state in order that it not interfere unduly with the private activities of religion, commerce, raising a family, and so forth. In some late nineteenth- and early twentieth-century accounts, emphasis is placed upon the positive role of the state in furthering individual material welfare as the condition for intellectual and political development. Even here, however, the first priority is not the functioning and harmony of the state or whole, but making possible the development of individual faculties to the point at which consent to obligation becomes commonsensically meaningful.

The most fundamental assumption of liberalism, usually implicit, seems to be the idea that "value is individual." This phrase of J. E. McTaggart goes some way, I believe, toward finding a common thread in what we have come to know as liberal theories of political life. It means that all judgments of good, bad, and worth must be made and judged for individuals as individuals, not as parts of wholes. (That this is only partially achievable is one reason, of course, that Aristotle's *Politics* has remained such a lively and relevant account.) And this view manifests itself in the requirement that political obligation arise from individual consent and, for some, that material goods be distributed on the basis of a matrix of individual economic choices.

Thus, the "individuality of value" implies that while concepts and tasks may ascend in generality and comprehend one another (as grand strategy comprehends diplomacy and tactics, for example), judgments of good, bad, and worth are not hierarchic in this fashion. Although the state may functionally comprehend the individual in some respects, it has no intrinsic worth in itself on this view, but is good or bad for individuals considered as such, whether philosophic or not, rather than first as contributors to, or participants in, political justice. This apolitical view has at least some of its origins in the teaching of Christ and the Stoics (which require no political mediation for moral redemption) as passed on by the medieval nominalism of the British Isles, and it has

been a test of skill of secular liberal theorists since Hobbes and
Locke to reconcile it with the commonsense value of preserving
the political association.

Thus, I am asking the reader to consider if there is not a
common assumption, explicit or otherwise, in accounts ranging
from the Hobbesian and Lockean states of nature to modern
defenses of economic freedom, and whether, if so, this may not
be the idea of the "individuality of value." Such a definition
might not please those within this tradition who are divided over
whether individuality is best nourished by adherence to formal
authority, or by a matrix of countervailing social and economic
passions, or by a tenacious assertion of the idea of natural rights
of acquisition. Yet this definition would serve to set all these
groups off from theorists for whom individuality and distinctness as high ends have not been thought interesting—Plato,
Aristotle, Cicero, St. Thomas Aquinas, Karl Marx, and some
modern socialists and scientists, for example. Nor would this
approach be at odds with those who have characterized the
liberal view as deriving political duties (such as they are) from
antecedent individual rights or passions, or prudential calculations about those passions. The individual starting point is required unless one is prepared to discuss the fundamental worth
of individuals as inseparable from some sort of whole—political,
social, natural, cosmic, and so forth. The criterion "individuality
of value" would exclude from "liberalism" only those theorists
claiming the label who start from a position that individual
judgments are beholden to the previous "social choices" of
others, and who begin, intentionally or not, to return to the
ancient view that the worth of nonphilosophic persons cannot be
discussed in abstraction from communities.

## 2

An interesting feature of Oakeshott's treatment of such matters
is its logical coherence. Oakeshott starts from an initial premise
that philosophy, as the investigation of conditions of intelligibility, has no direct bearing upon practical experience (the
realm of good, bad, and commonsense individuality), because
philosophy and practice are different mediations of experience
and have no common subject matter in a world in which all
experience, following Hegel, is mediate.[2] Oakeshott, in a Kantian
fashion with regard to the limits of reason,[3] can then be very

precise and direct in his theoretical accounts of civil and political matters, without concern that he will be led to undesired practical and political conclusions. Theoretical conclusions have no immediate consequences for practical life, and even in practical life, obligation to authority arises not solely from understanding, but from assent. (For Oakeshott, a theoretical syllogism could never validly conclude in a practical action.) The best political guide remains careful consideration of proposed policies and legislation in the light of the practices and traditions that are their wider context, with an eye and ear for what is "intimated," or tacitly acknowledged, or does not range so far from existing practices as to be unconvincing—the Victorian acceptance of bloomers but not shorts for bicycling, for example.[4] Here Oakeshott is clearly reminiscent of Hume, Burke, and the Roman or "conservative" inheritance in European politics.

Thus, Oakeshott can employ the terms "political" and "civil" in Aristotelian and Ciceronian fashion, to refer to the comprehensive or self-sufficient association,[5] without (unlike these ancients) attributing to the comprehensive association any intrinsic worth in a natural order. Obligation, for Oakeshott, is grounded in assent as a condition necessary to make understandable the idea of an individual moral agent, a theoretical creature necessary, because of the autonomy of his self-understandings, for the idea of civil association as formal association, as distinct from association to habituate certain specific responses.[6] Obligation here is not a promise to obey, but only acceptance of the procedures by which authority is constituted;[7] civil association is achieved in formal obligation that promises no substantial action. Since citizenship for most people is a fait accompli from birth, this seems to be the minimal civil condition to which one could subscribe without compromising one's status as a moral agent linking belief and action. The highest logical priority remains the integrity of the individual agent rather than the balance or health of the comprehensive association (which exists in the understandings of individual agents), because politics is human conduct, which requires the autonomy of self-understandings to occur.[8]

To link this abstraction to something more familiar, it can be seen that Oakeshott is close to Hobbes and Hume here in grounding individual freedom in a system of authority that demands little by way of promises of specific action. That is, Oakeshott distinguishes obligation, or *assent* to authority, from *approval* of the conditions of authority, and from a promise of *obedience*.

The practical effect of this abstraction, when it is achieved by citizens, is of course to preserve form and order in the body politic when there is little substantial agreement, or in times of crisis. Yet, for some, this entire discussion would be a distinction without a difference. Aristotelian and Platonic political science, for example, strongly grounded in the realm of sight and "the visible," simply cannot make sense of such Roman and Norman abstractions; and some of its modern proponents are prone to dismiss them as illusions susceptible of immoderate vulgarization.[9]

This is not a problem for Oakeshott, who, reflecting on historic European practices, spends some time showing that all specific actions and utterances are performed and made in terms of general practices or systems of meaning. Thus, to assent to a practice of authority is for Oakeshott somewhat like assenting to speak French while in France, as distinct from approving of the French language, or promising to say some specific sentence while speaking French. In fact, if a putative practice of authority included stipulations sufficiently specific as to be unambiguously performable in single actions, it would expose itself (in Oakeshott's lexicon) as an "instrumental" practice only masquerading as a "civil" practice. It would thereby reveal itself as an instance of a subcivil "enterprise association" formed to accomplish a substantial purpose like getting in the harvest, or putting out fires.[10] The freedom of citizens arises not so much in the silence but in the generality, of the laws or practices of authority; and obligation to a practice of authority is recognition of mutual subscription as the basis for the civil or comprehensive association. Without undue distortion, we may perhaps view all of this as Oakeshott's theoretical rendering of the European idea of civility as the tie among the diversity of human characters emerging from the medieval realms, a kind of fidelity more "watery," urbane, and moderate than those of a tribe, race, nation, or religion, or the "political friendship" of the polis (itself formed from tribes and villages).

Yet Oakeshott does retain from the Greek philosophers the ability to reason syllogistically. He is not guilty of using the words "civil" and "political" in the redundant and gratuitous fashion of many modern writers, who employ the terms to refer to economic or police functions without explaining what is logically distinctive about the idea of the "political." Consider, for example, Max Weber's well-known definition of the political association as the one that claims a legitimate monopoly of the means of physical force in a given territory. Weber's definition cannot logically distinguish the function of the political association from that of a mere police association or army, and thus leaves us the meaning of the word "political" still to seek. Or consider any of those engaged in the Baconian project of accumulating information and technology to "subdue nature," and who usually equate the state with an economy or a laboratory (filled with "role performers"). Not only do they fail to isolate a distinctively "political" or "civil" function, but they give weight to the charge that the entire vocabulary of justice is an illusion produced to disguise the material interests of the "stronger." The mark of "civil" and "political" must be their comprehensiveness if they are to remain unredundant.

In Oakeshott's account, the civil association comprehends or includes these narrower economic and police functions, and politics is the activity of attending to the general rules of this civil or comprehensive association. (There is no political association for Oakeshott—that would imply a return to the closer ties of the Greek *poleis*.) Thus, Oakeshott's use of "civil" may be seen to differ from that of Hegel and Marx, who, based on Rousseau's critique of Hobbes and Locke, used the expression "civil society" *(bürgerliche Gesellschaft)* to refer to economic life. And his account may be seen to differ from that of Hobbes and Locke in resisting the equation of civil association or society with the state or commonwealth, an institution achieved in the uneasy accommodation of "civil" and "enterprise" association.

The idea of civil association is also the idea of self-sufficient association for Oakeshott, because it has the formal purpose only of perpetuating recognition of itself as a legitimate system of authority, whereas police, economic, religious, and military associations all have some substantial purpose to accomplish. (Or, in the terms of Aristotle, they are done for the sake of something else.) Thus, they can never be self-sufficient activities, because their aim lies always outside of them in a realm of substantial actions that exhaust themselves in being accomplished, while civil association demands only an act of understanding (or misunderstanding) and assent. For example, a firehouse exhausts its purpose in putting out a fire, and is always dependent on something outside itself for perpetuation—another fire. Civil association, by contrast, may on occasion require the substantial action of putting out a fire, but accomplishment of this aim would not exhaust its purpose, which is higher in generality or more formal—the recognition of itself as a practice of authority to be taken into account in performing substantial actions.[11] "Civil" and "political" are distinguished by the comprehensiveness or generality of purpose to which they refer, and Oakeshott's vocabulary of politics remains meaningful or logically unredundant. We might also note here in passing that Oakeshott's combination of Roman and Greek ideas represents a logical advance over the Lockean account in the *Second Treatise*. Locke's account did not get beyond making the state or commonwealth the protector of private property as the resolution of the tension between the Latin "civil" and the Greek "political"; between the Roman association of private property holders and the Greek comprehensive ordering of citizens. Thus, Locke's account would not have escaped the Aristotelian charge that there is nothing distinctively political in economic and military associations to increase trade and provide security.

Not only philosophy, however, but also history is distinct from practical and political experience, and their judgments of worth or value, in Oakeshott's account of experience. Thus he permits another escape from the conceptual contortions that have tied up some liberal theorists. Conceiving of historical experience as the writing of a story in which the self-understandings and disclosures of individuals are recounted as the basis for explanation,[12] Oakeshott can give an account of the modern state, as it evolved in the understandings of various thinkers and historical actors, without equating it with a logical construct partially intimated in it—civil association. In other words, by writing two accounts of things civil and political,[13] one theoretical and one historical or contingent, Oakeshott is able to avoid dubious methodological and anthropological devices such as the "social contract" to account for the moral primacy of individual assent. His theoretical account of civil association, the artful synthesis of two millennia of diverse thoughts and visions, has no exact correspondence or necessary connection to the historic account of a modern European state, although it is intimated in certain passages of the modern state's history following the breakup of the medieval realm.

Briefly, Oakeshott suggests that the modern state has been understood along the lines of both civil association, or a practice of authority, and an "enterprise association," or corporation with a substantial purpose to accomplish: neither view has ever been able to silence the other completely, although the latter view is now clearly in the ascendant in a world replete with wars and crises.[14] In simpler language, this is to say that not everyone has

accepted the idea of civility as the basis for comprehensive
association; others have held tenaciously to the Baconian idea of
an association to conquer nature, and the latter view grows in
influence as it creates problems for which it claims to have the
only solutions.

To summarize thus far, I have tried to show that Oakeshott has
performed a service to political theorizing by demonstrating that
a logically coherent account of civil association as the comprehensive and self-sufficient association may be given that preserves both the Aristotelian idea of politics as the activity of
attending to the arrangements of the whole, and the liberal idea
of the individuality of value, as mediated by the Roman and
Norman idea of fidelity to authority as the bond among citizens. I
have suggested that this is an advance in logical coherence on
Locke, who bordered on equating civil association with an economic and military alliance to secure property, and thus made
civil association logically redundant. For Oakeshott, the freedom
of citizens arises not in the silence but in the generality of the
laws. And here is the glimmer of brilliance in the insight that it
was the achievement of the practice of civility that permitted the
European peoples to accommodate the feeling of the subjective
freedom of the individual personality with the ancient claim that
politics is concerned with the whole of life. There is also a
glimmer of brilliance in a theoretical articulation of this insight
as the idea that politics (as opposed to ruling and governance)
involves the formulation of *general* laws as the basis for civility
among individuals responding to these laws as they understand
(or misunderstand) them, and are obliged to them. One might say
that Rousseau and Hegel were on their way to this solution, but
that neither knew when to stop, and instead went on to make
such extravagant claims that their clearer insights were over-
shadowed.

## 3

At this point, however, critical attention may direct itself to the
question of Oakeshott's radical separation, even in analysis, of
philosophical, historical, and poetic experience, one from another, and from practical experience as the realm of good, bad,
and worth.[15] All of Oakeshott's modalities of experience are seen
as historic achievements, except for practical experience, which,
while not "necessary" is unavoidable.[16] One is compelled to ask

the basis for the separation of experience in this fashion. Are we simply a contingent unfolding of infinite forms of experience? Or is the whole account of experience (and politics) really a view from the poetic or aesthetic standpoint—a fleeting and purely formal image, created by a benevolent sorcerer with the practical intent of weakening the radical and imbalanced union of philosophy and politics in our time? If not, then where is the ballast in Oakeshott's account?

Oakeshott never addresses these questions systematically. He simply notes that, for whatever reasons, this is where we find ourselves, and implies by his silences that sufficient moderation is to be found in listening discerningly to the intimations of our traditions and general practices. Yet, it is precisely at this point that Oakeshott's theoretical account of both experience and civil association must be defended if it is to stand its philosophic ground. It would be possible here to lump Oakeshott's political thought facilely into the general category of Kantian liberalism (as a mere delineation of a formal, civil association to which rational individuals could consent) and argue that his treatment of practical experience, as distinct from philosophic exploration, stands or falls with a Humean or Kantian-like account of practical experience and practical reason, distancing the most fundamental ehtical questions from theoretical reason, which is permitted only to sketch their boundaries. Or, it would be possible, emphasizing passages about the continuity of historic practices, to treat Oakeshott's writings as merely a more sophisticated version of Burkean liberalism (with fewer political examples!). But I believe that to cast Oakeshott's thought in this or that narrow mold, and cart it out only on certain occasions, would be to cheat ourselves of something very interesting. As I am seeking to show, the implied defense in Oakeshott's few philosophic claims is to be found in their ability to produce a coherent account of the civil and political aspects of modern individualism.

Consider, as part of this demonstration, Oakeshott's critique of what he calls modern "rationalism"—"the most remarkable intellectual fashion of post-Renaissance Europe."[17] It confusedly attempts to separate the form and content of specific knowledge and craft in the formulation of a universal method applicable to all subject matters;[18] in the fashion, for example, of the modern pseudoscientific enterprise to reduce all academic disciplines to the methods of modern physics. As Oakeshott sees it, the attempt to separate the "how" from the "what" of any concrete knowledge and put it in books and techniques is an illusion that, over time, results in the loss of genuine skill. The "how" and "what," the form and content, of any concrete activity arise simultaneously and reciprocally, and can be separated only in the irrelevance and loss of fluid skill evident, for instance, in the politics of our age.

This critique of modern rationalism is consistent with Oakeshott's general account of experience and its modalities. The distinctness of the various modes of experience—practice, history, science, poetry—arises because they have no common subject matter beyond "raw" experience unknowable except in specific mediation. The form and content of each (as experiential possibilities) arises in a give-and-take between the absolute claims of each, which over time achieves a recognizable and coherent way of mediating experience. (In this sense, we might say that the "prototype" for all experience, in Oakeshott's account, is poetic experience, which collapses into fleeting, unified instants the content and form of specific thoughts and experiences.)[19] Because there is nothing outside of experience on this view, the modalities of practice, poetry, science, and history can never address one another except in a kind of "social" conversation where each is admitted for what it appears to be, since, carefully speaking, they have nothing in common to talk about, according to Oakeshott.[20] There are, in brief, no transferable forms of experience or activity.

At a practical level, we find a similar teaching in the ethics of Aristotle, the philosopher of "common sense," who tells us that an intelligent man will always choose a method appropriate to his subject matter.[21] This is the basis for Aristotle's choice of a rough dialectic method (over a precise one) for expositing the activity of politics, a branch of moral action. Aristotle obviously did not accept the notion of a universal method for all subjects, but on the other hand, he could never have accepted with consistency something like Oakeshott's account of experience and its various mediations, presupposing the tension between "subject" and "object" as the primary datum of something called "experience." Aristotle clearly believed that the unchanging order of the world was accessible to the intellective faculty when this was correctly tutored, since the intellect was part of this order, and also contained it.[22] A question then arises whether, although Oakeshott's account of experience is consistent with his practical teaching about the inseparability of method and subject matter, it is logically necessary as a basis for it.

The answer appears to be that it *is* logically necessary, and here can be seen something intelligent that Oakeshott has preserved from Aristotle for an indivdualist age that could probably not recover Aristotle's understanding of man's natural ends. Surveying a century littered with the débris of "rationalist" political projects, Oakeshott is concerned to explain what is amiss. Simply to say to his world (as he does in footnotes) that it has combined the worst of ancient and medieval claims for "Reason"—broad scope and scholastic rigidity, respectively[23]—will not go very far in getting attention. And so Oakeshott has taken his practical bearings from something all can appreciate, a Socratic starting point of sorts—skill in crafts. Oakeshott can agree with the Athenian philosophers that skill is acquired and preserved through patient apprenticeship, but his explanation of why this is so is very different, because he sees no natural ends from within a *psyche* that contains and recollects them.

For an age with predominantly "nominalist" assumptions—that there are meanings in the mind, and things in the world—there is always the danger of too much abstraction, the danger of meanings and things getting too far apart. This is what Oakeshott calls the error of modern Rationalism—the illusion that it can rationally devise systems or techniques from makeshift parts and apply them universally without effective limits. Oakeshott endeavors to show that when practical action is skillful, this is not what actually happens, even if it is conceived in these terms. Rather, in Oakeshott's account of experience and skill, both the form and content of any concrete activity arise simultaneously and creatively, and we are not at liberty to trade them around like pieces of a mechanical puzzle, without paying a price. Oakeshott's account is in agreement with the Aristotelian insight that gaps or leaps in the steps of any concrete knowledge produce immoderation, especially in politics and governance. And Oakeshott has given an account of this practical insight for an age that has lost an understanding of itself as part of a nature that would divulge these insights in the proper intellective progression.

**4**

Another comparison of Oakeshott with Aristotle may help us to decide if Oakeshott has said something interesting, or simply presented us with an illusion of sorts. Is it possible that the

context for politics, the comprehensive or self-sufficient association, be formal association with no extrinsic or substantial purpose to accomplish?

Oakeshott implies (in a mood reminiscent of Hegel's leaps
from the implicit to the explicit) that Aristotle was on his way to
what he, Oakeshott, has in mind by civil association.[24] But, in
spite of his attempts to minimize them, there are clearly important differences between Aristotle's account and Oakeshott, not
only over the purposes of the self-sufficient association, but over
the relation of the intellectual and moral virtues to politics as
well. Most importantly, politics for Aristotle was not "human
conduct," an interior Stoic realm of choices not causes; and the
regime was not a neutral authority separate from the holders of
power. Aristotelian politics, even in the mixed regime, involved
not primarily individual understandings and misunderstandings, but habituation to the best way of life which the circumstances permitted. Political (not civil) association was natural for
Aristotle because it reflected and enhanced the happy actualiza-
tion of the potentials of hierarchic and interlocking natural
human faculties, the pinnacle of which was pure intellect—the
only eternal part of the *psyche*, and the only principle of action
capable of performance solely for its own sake.[25]

Now, I want to try to show here that Oakeshott's idea of assent
to a practice of authority (as distinct from approving of it, or
promising to obey it) would have been unintelligible or illusory
for Aristotle (though perhaps not for Cicero). Oakeshott can make
this distinction, and we can follow him in it, because it was a
distinction achieved by some of our medieval predecessors. Yet
they achieved it by cultivating a faculty of the soul known as the
will, a faculty opaque to the light of the intellect, and capable of
opposing (without pathology) the conclusions of reasoning. By
contrast, if the "beings" of the world were given in the *psyche*, as
Aristotle said, then the idea of assent to a practice of authority
detached from substantial actions would be simply nonsense.
Oakeshott's account requires an abstract faculty in humans
which can know certain general rules or meanings, yet still
choose to subscribe to others without illusion or philosophic
irrelevance. Or, it at least requires the civilized residue of that
insight in the understandings of his secular audience, if the
account is to make sense of their experience. Oakeshott's account
of civil association falls somewhere between what he calls in one
essay the traditions of "Will and Artifice" and the "Rational
Will."[26]

We must also ask whether Oakeshott's theoretical articulation of historic European political practice sheds light on the activities of rule and politics beyond that provided by Aristotle's reflection on the Greek city-states. My judgment is that it does, because it systematizes and draws out (as well) Roman ideas and words about civil and public life, and the Romans showed more of a genius for rule and governance than did the Athenians.

The general shortcoming of the politics of the Greek *poleis*, and the systematic reflection on it by Plato and Aristotle, was arguably the failure to achieve a clear idea and practice of authority, distinguished from the balance of power at any moment. A regime or constitution for Aristotle was an ordering of citizens in a specific way, and the "state" changed when the ordering of citizens changed.[27] The key to political stability in Athenian political science was psychic harmony in citizens, or a balance of power deriving from psychic balance in at least one segment of the citizens, in many cities. Thucydides' implied criticism of his fellow Athenians in *The Peloponnesian War*, for example, seems to have been precisely that they were imbalanced through too much daring, and of the Spartans that they were imbalanced through too little daring.[28] The instability of Greek politics, then, seems to have derived in part from the inability to achieve a faculty of the personality (like the "will") capable of assenting to a constitutional characteristic known to the Roman and European tradition as *authority*, distinguished from the actual ordering of the citizens at any moment, or from the political programme, or governance, of the oligarchs, the democrats, and so forth. The Roman idea of fidelity to the authority of its practices, inseparably bound to its civil religion (and well appreciated by that Greek ambassador, Polybius), achieved a stability which gave the Roman constitution, in all its mutations, a longevity absent from the Athenian.

# 5

Over a period of two millennia, the European peoples managed to combine both Christian and re-discovered Greek ideas within the Roman and Germanic governmental institutions and practices they inherited. In the passage of that history known as modern liberalism, systematic reflection on politics usually proceeded by accounting for the freedom of individuals in the silence of the law, in the fashion of Hobbes and (to some degree)

Locke. Until Hegel, it seems to have resisted the Aristotelian idea of politics as the art of attending to the comprehensive associa- tion, of balancing the claims of the other arts and sciences, because this would appear to conflict with the claims of individ- ual freedom, and later, self-expression. It might have made cit- izens the mere "matter" of a political craft or techne. But Hegel, in the end, was too much of a "rationalist" to permit the exten- sion of the claims of nonphilosophic freedom to extend beyond the realm of the "personality."

Oakeshott, however, has managed to combine the Aristotelian claim for politics as the practical art of attending to the arrange- ments of the comprehensive association with the requirements of individuality, by simply noting that assent to the authority of general laws (versus commands or directives) leaves room for both ideas, and in both theory and practice. That is, the freedom of citizens (versus role performers) arises in acts of individual judgment subsuming particular policies under general laws, like deriving a policy of conscription from the requirement to provide for the common defense. Assent to the authority of general laws is the only quality that could be assented to without promises of substantial action that would make the general relationship of civility impossible. Nor is Oakeshott's account here sharply at odds with the Aristotelian requirement that political association teach moral virtues, so long as these virtues or habits can be nourished by laws sufficiently general to be incapable of specify- ing particular actions, and thus still require acts of individual judgment to be operative. Nor is Oakeshott forced to the logically extreme (and politically immoderate) position of asserting, like Rousseau and Kant, that we are "free" in obeying a law that we give to ourselves. The "creative" act (not his language) for Oakeshott is restricted to the assent to authority postulated if we assume the freedom of reflective consciousness in civil associ- ates.

I am unable to see that any other theorist of modern liberalism has given as coherent an explanation as Oakeshott of the diverse historical inheritances in its political experience. And, while hoping to evade the ghost of Hegel, I would venture to suggest, in addition, that Oakeshott's theoretical account of modern Euro- pean political practices and reflection issues in insights that reiterate the relevance of Aristotle's account for modern politics, while indicating its limitations for an individualist age, sepa- rated from Aristotle by Roman law, and persuaded by coherence in systems of willfully created concepts, rather than intellective conjunction with the "beings that are."

To avail ourselves of the lucid insights of Athenian political science about psychic and political equilibrium in the different kinds of human beings ("spirited," or "appetitive," for instance) will become more relevant to governance in our Western societies as they become even more democratic, or materialist and egalitarian. These insights are an important political resource in our inheritance from the past. To remember and recover the insights of our more abstract and politically talented Roman and Norman forebears[29] about the authority of law and its place in rule and governance will also become more relevant as we find our populaces in periods of sufficient political disequilibrium that Athenian (and Tocquevillean) equilibrium techniques will no longer check further disorder. Prudent political practice will involve knowing when to tap which inherited resource, and how to incorporate both in the self-understanding of a liberal world of discourse.

1985

## Notes

1. Michael J. Oakeshott, "On the Character of a Modern European State," in *On Human Conduct* (Oxford: Clarendon Press, 1975), 245, n. 2; and "The Rule of Law," in *On History* (Oxford: Basil Blackwell, 1983), 162. Oakeshott implies that this development has flowed in part from Locke's having made the executive rather than the judicial the power responsible for the execution of the laws, a blurring of the medieval distinction between the realms of *jurisdictio* and *gubernaculum*, of rights and policy. Over time, the welfare of citizens was affirmed as a proper object of policy.

2. In the sense that all experience is had in modality, and there is nothing outside of experience (Michael J. Oakeshott, *Experience and Its Modes* [Cambridge University Press, 1933], 17–18).

3. The practical effect of the separation of practice as the realm of good and bad, from philosophy as the investigation of conditions of intelligibility, is similar to the effect of Kant's separation of the noumenal and phenomenal realms—the most fundamental ethical questions become ultimately inaccessible to theoretical reason. See Oakeshott, *Experience and Its Modes*, 1.

4. Michael J. Oakeshott, "Rational Conduct," in *Rationalism in Politics* (London: Methuen, 1962), 95–96.

5. Michael J. Oakeshott, "On the Civil Condition," in *On Human Conduct*, 110.

6. Ibid., 112.

7. Ibid., 163.

8. Ibid., 164.

9. Consider the concern in the works of Leo Strauss and his students for the dangers of "abstraction from the body" in politics. This insight is an important corrective for some of the utopian projects of our time (and even disarms somewhat the charges of radical feminism about the abstraction of masculine thought). But by apparently taking its bearings almost exclusively from the most obvious abuse of authority in recent history, this school of thought risks not bringing to attention in its pedagogy the importance for civil and political order of one particular abstraction—assent to the authoritative procedures by which law is made.

10. Oakeshott, "On the Civil Condition," in *On Human Conduct*, 114–17.

11. Ibid., 147.

12. Michael J. Oakeshott, "On the Theoretical Understanding of Human Conduct," in *On Human Conduct*. 104–07.

13. That is, the second and third essays, respectively, of *On Human Conduct*—"On the Civil Condition" and "On the Character of a Modern European State."

14. Oakeshott, "On the Character of a Modern European State," 272–74.

15. Oakeshott, *Experience and Its Modes*. 311.

16. Ibid., chap. 5.

17. Oakeshott, "Rationalism in Politics," 1.

18. Ibid., 8. See also Wendell J. Coats, Jr., "Michael Oakeshott and the Character of Experience" (unpublished doctoral dissertation, University of Michigan Microfilms, 1978). 245.

19. Michael J. Oakeshott, "The Voice of Poetry in the Conversation of Mankind," in *Rationalism in Politics*, 246. See also *Experience and Its Modes*, 297, for Oakeshott's early view that art and poetry occurred within practical experience: and the "Preface" to *Rationalism in Politics*.

20. Oakeshott, "The Voice of Poetry," 202.

21. Aristotle, *Nicomachean Ethics*, book I, chap. 3.

22. Aristotle, *De Anima*. book III.

23. Oakeshott, *Rationalism in Politics*, 16–18.

24. Oakeshott, "On the Civil Condition," 110. But compare with Aristotle, *Politics*, book III, chap. 9, on the ties among citizens.

25. Aristotle, *De Anima*, book III.

26. Michael J. Oakeshott, "Introduction" to Thomas Hobbes, *Leviathan*, ed. by Michael J. Oakeshott (Oxford: Basil Blackwell, 1946), xii.

27. Aristotle, *Politics*, book III, chap. 3.

28. The point is that most of Thucydides' analysis of the war is in terms of psychological balance and balance of power.

29. See, in this connection, Oakeshott, "On the Rule of Law," 164; and Sir Henry Pollock and Frederick Maitland, *The History of English Law* (Cambridge: Cambridge University Press, 1898), book I, chaps. 3–5.

# The Ideology of Arms Control

The antinuclear movement portrays Americans as confronted in the nuclear age with a stark choice between peace and all-out nuclear war. Indeed, the movement's appeal has flowed in large part from the dramatic clarity with which its leaders have posed this choice for the public. Yet contrary to the impression sometimes conveyed by the movement's spokesmen, this way of viewing the problem is not new. Far from articulating a fresh departure in American thinking about nuclear arms, the outlook of the peace movement can be said to represent the logical culmination of a doctrine that has dominated U.S. strategic thinking for the past twenty years—a doctrine in no small measure responsible for the dilemma in which we now find ourselves. At its heart, the stance of the peace movement is a reformulation of the modern ideology of arms control, which has always sought to avert war by narrowing the alternatives to a choice between nuclear war and peace.[1]

From the outset, the overriding problem with arms control doctrine has been the divergence between U.S. and Soviet views of the problem posed by nuclear weapons. In the 1960s, the United States abandoned for its conventional force the goal of victory in war on the grounds that such a goal would destabilize the nuclear "balance of terror." Conventional forces were to be used only as a catalyst to negotiations. It followed that they must never be victorious in any decisive sense but rather that they should simply force us back to the alternatives of nuclear war or peace. By the late 1970s, it had become apparent to a number of American observers that the Soviet Union had never accepted this formulation of the military alternatives available to a nation in the nuclear age. Soviet military doctrine continued to permit its conventional forces to aim at decisive victory in tactical operations, and thus the Soviets were able to justify a continuing

This article first appeared in the *Journal of Contemporary Studies* 5, no. 3 (Summer 1982): 5–15. Permission to reprint it here is gratefully acknowledged.

conventional and nuclear arms buildup. The Soviets persisted in pursuing a third alternative—defeat of Western forces and dissolution of Western political will short of nuclear war. What is of interest here is not the Soviet view, which is quite traditional, but the American view that victory is an obsolete idea.[2] How did we come to this view of all (peace) or nothing (spasm nuclear war), but never victory?

## The Arms Control Logic

The doctrine of arms control has implied from the beginning an entire perspective on national security.[3] Under the arms control perspective, the emergence of nuclear weapons is seen to have rendered obsolete the traditional conception of the defense of the state as understood from the time of Xenophon to that of Clausewitz. In the view of arms controllers, the use of force, directed toward disintegration of an opposing political will, and structured by the idea of victory—that is, superior mass at a decisive point in time and space—is no longer a serious possibility at any operational level. Because nuclear war is not winnable for any side, national security (in lieu of national defense) must be based upon avoiding the use of nuclear weapons—a goal attained by deterring large-scale aggression through the credible threat of unacceptable, punitive retaliation.

Because no sane administration in either the United States or the Soviet Union (the smaller countries are a different problem) would ever intentionally initiate nuclear war, the gravest threat facing all of us is the possibility of accidental nuclear war, arising from the breakdown of communications, misperception of intentions, or loss of political will and authority. Whereas for past ages the future was always uncertain, in the nuclear age certainty must become a major goal. Technical assurances, insulated insofar as possible from human error, must be found in order to guarantee that nuclear weapons will never be used. The delicate balance of terror must be kept stable by the establishment of essentially equal weapons levels on both sides through ongoing negotiations aimed at commensurate weapons reductions.

Use of military force in limited areas is permitted, but only for the purpose of returning concerned powers to the negotiating table, where collective bargaining can resume. Any use of force for traditional military goals such as victory or local territorial control is "destabilizing" of the nuclear arms balance and could link together a chain of events leading to an essentially "accidental," all-out nuclear war. In short, like the Hobbesian political theory based upon fear of violent death, United States security policy must continually take its bearings from the worst-case hypothesis—the possibility of accidental nuclear war leading to the destruction of, at least, Western civilization.

This viewpoint had direct policy effects from the mid-1960s, under Secretary of Defense Robert McNamara, through the early 1970s, under Secretary of Defense James Schlesinger. It is still a very influential point of view, although parts of it are not popular with the Reagan administration. As a policy perspective, arms control doctrine can account for a number of various and apparently unrelated developments in United States defense policy since the mid-1960s.

To begin with, it can account for the shape and composition of our nuclear forces with intercontinental range. On most of our land- and submarine-based ICBMs we have relatively small warheads, initially intended to be used against cities, not against other missiles. Cities can be destroyed with smaller weapons than are necessary to destroy hardened missile silos. In the view of arms controllers, to have built large warheads or highly accurate guided missiles would have been destabilizing of the nuclear arms balance because it would have provided us with the capability actually to *defend* the country, properly speaking, rather than simply to assure an unacceptable, "punitive" second strike. (In other words, in the logic of the arms controllers, it might have led to the use of the weapons.) In addition, the several hundred B-52 bombers that make up the third leg of our triad of nuclear forces are now so old (more than two decades) that most U.S. Air Force pilots train in computer simulators to extend the life of the planes. The canceling of the new B-1 bomber in 1977 was consistent with the arms controllers' view that bombers are highly destabilizing due to the fact that they can be sent out to threaten and then be called back, thus contributing to the kind of misunderstanding that might lead to accidental nuclear war. Even the placing of multiple warheads (MIRVs) on our Minuteman III missiles was consistent with the arms controllers' requirement for technical assurances that the weapons will never be used. If you put several warheads on one missile, it follows that you cannot afford to let it remain in its silo during attack. Thus, your opponent is assured of your instantaneous retaliation, and supposedly does not attack in the first place.

The failure to develop means to protect the American people

against attack by nuclear weapons is also consistent with arms control doctrine. The absence of any serious civil defense and complete lack of ballistic missile defense, is a product of the view that the ability to defend your population against nuclear attack is itself destabilizing. Stability is best preserved by the mutual assurance of your own and the opposition's destruction. To maintain shelters might encourage the belief that nuclear war could actually be fought: better to leave your population un- protected and thus assure that you can never use the weapons without the destruction of the American people. One con- sequence of this posture is the almost automatic assurance of political opposition to any leader who dares to confront or finds it necessary to create an atmosphere of confrontation.[4]

## Arms Control and Vietnam

Our conduct of the war in Vietnam is also illuminated by the logic of arms control. Fighting was directed by economic models. The aim was to inflict pain upon the enemy incrementally, up to a point of diminishing marginal returns on our investment in lives and money. Our handling of the war made plain to the whole world that American firepower would be used only to bring the concerned powers back to the negotiating table, where collective bargaining techniquess would be used to solve dif- ferences. There was never a serious attempt to achieve victory in the traditional sense or to undertake the measures that victory would have required, such as sustained interdiction of enemy supply lines outside of South Vietnam and consolidation of territorial gains. All these measures would have been, in the arms control model, destabilizing of the nuclear arms balance and might even have mobilized American sentiment behind the war. The trick was to walk a tightrope betwen mounting American casualties and formulation of serious war aims.

The logic of arms control can also account for changes over the past fifteen years in American tactical doctrine, away from the idea of victory in the land battle as the basis for tactical opera- tions, toward the view of warfare based on the technical problem of "targeting."[5] Behind this shift lies the view that war is ul- timately a technical, not a practical or strategic, problem. Again, according to arms control logic, the idea of victory as a guide for the conduct of operations is destabilizing of the nuclear arms balance. It encourages a broad perspective and the tendency to link the use of force to attainment of political goals. Preferred is a compartmentalized, technical approach to warfare viewed as simply a series of discrete problems in targeting, going nowhere in particular (except toward mounting casualties).

The effects of arms control policy can also account for the general ill-repute into which U.S. armed services have fallen, at least until the present administration. In brief, the real enemy becomes one's own military forces, because they are the ones likely to escalate hostilities and call up the specter of all-out nuclear war. At the same time, they are expected to perform certain minimal military functions. Yet because conventional forces cannot be allowed to attempt victory by massing decisive force, but instead must serve only to pressure adversaries into negotiations, in the end they must always lose. Thus they are caught in a double bind: when they lose, they fall into disrepute; but if they show signs of winning they are feared, for then they threaten to escalate the conflict into nuclear instability.[6] Finally, when negotiations themselves force another "graduated" U.S. withdrawal because (1) in our own doctrine we cannot afford to leave the bargaining table without a settlement lest we be guilty of destabilization, and (2) we generally refuse to pressure opponents with military force once negotiations begin, the disrespect originally attached to the uniformed military spreads to the government's diplomacy as well.[7]

Finally, the prevalence of the arms control perspective in and out of government can make sense of three otherwise puzzling recent developments: (1) the rejection of the SALT II treaty (which could never have been accomplished by conservatives alone); (2) "Presidential Directive 59," which authorizes targeting of Soviet military and Communist party command structures; and (3) recent calls for conventional troop buildups in NATO as a substitute for deployment of intermediate-range nuclear weapons in the European theater.[8] The key to the puzzle is the requirement for an *assured* second-strike capability to inflict unacceptable damage on an aggressor and thus deter aggression.

The development and production of over three hundred large, new Soviet missiles (SS-18s)—made very accurate through sale of American ball-bearing technology, and soon to be armed with up to ten large warheads apiece—threatens the land-based U.S. Minuteman force, the bulk of our second-strike capability. Because the SS-18 missiles were permitted the Soviets under SALT II, those arms controllers who accepted the argument that our second-strike capability was threatened or made less credible could and did oppose the treaty. To allow our own retaliatory force to become vulnerable is to generate instability in the nuclear arms balance by *inviting* attack. Also permitted within the arms control framework was a publicly articulated targeting doctrine directed toward Soviet Communist party and military targets, making punitive, second-strike retaliatory capability credible in the face of the SS-18 threat. (This is still not the same as building larger, accurate missiles capable of destroying Soviet missiles in their silos.)

The recent arguments to forego upgrading NATO intermediate-range nuclear capabilities in Western Europe, and go to a stated "no first-use" nuclear weapons policy while strengthening conventional forces, are also consistent with the arms control perspective. Such missiles in Western Europe, which could reach Soviet targets in six to eight minutes, will make the Soviets nervous about their own second-strike capability and generally destabilize the nuclear arms balance, on this view. The call for strengthened conventional forces in NATO still suggests no traditional military uses for them, such as trying to win the land battle. Conventional forces are intended primarily to "stretch out" the time for negotiations to end incipient hostilities (most likely through further U.S. accommodation) and thereby to avoid the use of nuclear weapons. This move also aims to placate the European and American peace movements. The point, in arms control, is to get domestic populations to see the alternatives as nuclear war or peace, so that they will put pressure on their political leaders not to confront or escalate—while maintaining a sense of moderation that prevents the same domestic populations from becoming so excited or frenzied that they contribute to instability through sustained unpredictability or even demands for complete, unilateral disarmament.

To summarize, arms control aims to be a full national security policy for the nuclear age. It substitutes the idea of security, through technical assurances and formal weapons agreements issuing from international collective bargaining, for the idea of defense *per se* as the capability to eliminate the adversary's ability to commence or continue hostilities. In short, it attempts to substitute a technical solution (assured retaliation and arms reductions) for what is essentially a political problem, arguing that the possibility of accidental nuclear war makes this a necessity. Displays of resolve and political will must not be permitted, because they might establish the destabilizing link between force and national sovereignty. Finally, by linking the conduct of local military operations to the chain of events that *could* set off accidental nuclear war, it forces both U.S. diplomacy and military policy continually to take their bearings from a possible worst-case scenario.

Yet the new science of arms control is making a serious miscalculation about how to avoid the instability that might lead to use of nuclear weapons. In its obsession with absolute certainty and control, it is backing into the very thing it has sought to avoid—destabilization of the nuclear arms balance. Although the goal of deterring the use of nuclear weapons is worthy, the accompanying loss of nerve (reflected in the attempt by arms control advocates to eliminate the political resolve in American leadership that might lead to confrontation with the Soviets) is contributing to a genuinely destabilizing loss of American practical military and diplomatic skill. Not only is this worrisome in the face of a continuing Soviet nuclear and conventional arms buildup, but it forebodes the enervation of political will and resolve in American politics—a development that Alexis de Tocqueville repeatedly warned us to guard against if we would preserve our political freedom as we become more democratic. I shall begin with the discussion of our loss of practical military and diplomatic skill and then take up the problem of our paralysis of political will. Although I believe the former derives initially from the latter, after a time they begin to feed (or starve) one another.

## Critique of Arms Control

Each profession has its own ends and means. Although there is some room for tinkering with the means of a profession—for instance, exchanging one tool for another—there is not much latitude for altering ends or general goals without fundamentally altering the original profession or replacing it with something else. Furthermore, the attempt to change the end of a profession without changing its means can result in loss of practical skill as the profession wrestles with the problem of determining its fundamental purposes. Something like this happened as arms controllers tried to change the end of the military profession to the civil police function of keeping order in South Vietnam, while continuing to demand from it the sacrifices associated with military, not civil police, duties.

Until the new science of arms control, the aim of the military profession was to provide the nation with the least inhumane solution to external problems of force by developing and practicing the expertise necessary to dissolve the ability and will of the opposing force to continue hostilities. The basis of this expertise was tactics, the art of fire and maneuver directed toward massing superior force at a decisive point in time and space known as victory. The art of tactics saw itself as providing a way to end hostilities skillfully and short of eliminating the entire opposing force (and the civilian population it defended). Although tactical operations were conducted with loss of life, the losses were redeemed by translating military sacrifice through strategy into meaningful political achievements.

In addition to this emotional requirement, especially in the face of mounting casualties, there was a practical and even logical reguirement for the idea of victory. It was the goal that ordered all the other efforts. All principles of fire and maneuver, whether direct or indirect, were ultimately directed toward massing force to break the enemy's will and ability to continue to fight. It is not clear that anything else has ever been able to justify in men's minds the kinds of sacrifices war demands. (Can even mercenaries be expected to fight for long in the face of mounting casualties without the motivation of political goals?) Once an army begins to take casualties it is forced into either (1) withdrawal, (2) surrender, or (3) offensive actions to eliminate the ability of the opposing force to continue hostilities. Yet under the arms controllers' direction, almost all powers fighting the United States have become relatively equal to it, because we refuse to take the offensive on grounds that it is destabilizing. Thus, we can only accept losses and continue to withdraw militarily and diplomatically.

## Victory vs. "Body Count"

It is instructive to scrutinize the confusion of ends involved in the direction of the Vietnam war by arms controller Defense Secretary McNamara and his advisors. Given the overriding goal of avoiding nuclear war, the argument was made that military science could no longer be the science of victory, because the resulting escalation might lead to expanded hostilities with the People's Republic of China or the Soviet Union, and eventually to the use of nuclear weapons. Yet, initially anyway, there was a desire to wield influence in Southeast Asia to check the expansion of the North Vietnamese communists and their proxies in South Vietnam. This meant that force would be used in a limited and controlled way to inflict pain incrementally in expectation of "marginal" political gains. Although use of force was to be limited, there was still a need for some way to measure "success," short of victory. This led to a measure of "military" success that was able to be quantified and controlled by the science of ecnomics—the "body count," dramatized nightly on television screens across America as a legitimate military aim. Additionally, arms control introduced logical muddle into the military vocabulary so that theory would not contradict practice. The words "strategic" and "tactical" were redefined as budgeting categories, the former referring to funding for nuclear weapons with intercontinental ranges. Formerly, the relationship between strategy and tactics had been hierarchic, strategy referring to the art of linking together tactical or local successes in such a way as to defeat the enemy forces. Now the logical link between the two had been severed and the terms given technical, compartmentalized meanings with no special connection to one another.

In brief, the arms controller calculated that the way to prevent escalation of military activity in Vietnam was to induce mutation of the defining principles of the U.S. military profession. (It is far from evident that any communist army has been willing to accept the arms controllers' view of tactics.) The link joining tactics, strategy, and victory was severed, and the body count was introduced as a new measure of military success. The effect on the professional U.S. officer corps (and in turn on the conscript army and the American people) was devastating. In short, the purpose of the military profession was debased. Rather than attempt to achieve victory through application of tactical expertise, commanders were expected to kill as many of the enemy as possible.[9] Morale, self-esteem, and military effectiveness all suffered as a result.

The drop in military effectiveness was ultimately a consequence of the faulty and incomplete presuppositions of the economic approach to warfare employed by the arms controllers. Instead of looking at human nature as they found it, these men argued backwards from what they considered to be the moral imperative of our times—the necessity to avoid any development that might lead, even accidentally, to the use of nuclear weapons. Human beings would be changed because they had to be changed. A method of employing force in a graduated fashion would simply be imposed universally upon the human psyche: if we killed enough Viet Cong gradually, the will of surviving Viet Cong would diminish, commensurately. But *homo economics* is not the whole man. There is still in us the "spiritedness" spoken of by Plato's Socrates—this thing in people that, when properly channeled, will drive them to make all sorts of sacrifices for political goals beyond any calculus of utility. Thus the "graduated" infliction of casualties on the Viet Cong simply heightened their resolve to fight.

If this had been done in a decisive and sustained way, in combination with serious interdiction of enemy supply lines outside of South Vietnam, it might conceivably have resulted in a U.S. military victory. But this was not what the arms controllers had in mind, for it would have been an admission and allowance of "spiritedness" and political resolve on our part, a destabilizing eruption: The economic psychology of the arms control model will not admit the existence of a part of human beings not subject to incremental measurement and control, because this would be to concede an impermissible uncertainty in human affairs in the age of nuclear weapons.[10] Yet spiritedness persists in the human breast despite the efforts of arms controllers, and when U.S. casualties began to mount in Vietnam, the spiritedness and political resolve that were not permitted to erupt on the battlefield erupted, as it were, back home in the form of protest *against* the war.

The effects of antiwar protest at home, the limited success on the battlefield (combined with steady casualties), and the arms control approach to bargaining in general all congealed to lessen our diplomatic effectiveness in negotiating even a measured withdrawal during the Nixon presidency. Yet the drama itself unfolded within the script initially written and directed by the arms controllers. Avoidance of nuclear war requires that we avoid confrontation or demonstrations of political resolve. Thus all differences must be open to negotiated settlements; not to reach a settlement is itself destabilizing of the nuclear arms balance. Armed force will be used only to return adversaries to the negotiating table, not to pressure them once they are negotiating, however outrageous or uncompromising their demands. In time, the direction of diplomatic negotiations parallels the direction of events on the battlefield—graduated withdrawal and concessions, with flashes of resolve permitted only to stop a complete rout (itself destabilizing). There is a cumulative and reciprocal loss of military and diplomatic skill and effectiveness as both professions are forced to take their bearings continually from avoidance of any action that might conceivably destablize the nuclear arms balance. (This approach to bargaining reappears in the unequal terms of SALT II. Because in our own models we could not afford *not* to reach a settlement, we were continually ratifying the Soviet arms buildup, especially in the form of the SS-18 missiles and the Backfire bomber.)

The requirement for absolute certainty and control over all facets of external policy in the interest of avoiding accidental nuclear war, manifested in the attempt to eliminate anything resembling spirited independence and resolve, not only results in our doing poorly in activity requiring the ability to confront (e.g., tactics and diplomacy) but also augurs ill for the future of political freedom in America. It was Tocqueville who, in alerting us to the conflict between freedom and equality, warned that expanding equality might well lead to a loss of political balance and resolve as we were pulled more and more into the realm of things that can be equalized—material comforts. The hope of preserving our political resolve, according to Tocqueville, lay in preserving the tension between the democratic desire for material comfort and formal institutions requiring public-spiritedness. Tocqueville suggested that our political will might gradually be enervated or slackened as we slid into a kind of benign, unspirited, materialistic despotism. If we cherish political freedom, he cautioned, we must preserve our political will and resolve. Could Tocqueville have foreseen that it would be a variation on the Hobbesian theme of fear of violent death in the form of arms control doctrine that might exponentially advance the enervation of our political will?

## Need for a New Policy

Spiritedness—this opaque, irrational force in us that makes us angry, and when properly channeled makes us courageous and lead us to make sacrifices of comfort and even life for family, friends, and country—has always been the political "problem." Whatever its dangers, it is also the basis of our political freedom because it propels us to fight tyranny, or the desire of others to dominate us. Arms control doctrine has chosen to ignore this part of the human psyche and base its calculations on those of our motivations that can be controlled and directed with certainty, treating all motivations as variations of consumer demands, subject to the laws of economic rationality. Perhaps the arms controllers believe privately that spiritedness, and political orientation in general, can and must be unlearned if we are to achieve the stability necessary to survive the nuclear age. And perhaps in private they might admit that some loss of political resolve and freedom is a small price to pay to avoid nuclear war.

But what if they are wrong, as I believe they are, about how to avoid nuclear war? What if the economic psychology on which their model is predicated is faulty and partial? What if political resolve and spiritedness cannot be unlearned at all? Or, what if they can be partially tamed or unlearned, but unlearning them on one side (ours) while not on the other side contributes to instability? In short, how are we to deal with the Soviet SS-18 threat bequeathed us by the arms controllers in such a way as to maintain a stable balance of power?

We might begin by formulating a foreign and defense policy predicated on the understanding that spiritedness is a part of our humanity, and that to avoid nuclear war we must *work with* political resolve, not attempt to exterminate it. To open the way for such a policy, it is first necessary to sever the mythical, automatic link in our policy thinking between instability in the nuclear arms balance and the conduct of tactical operations with conventional forces, and to allow the directing idea of victory to again form the basis for tactics. There is nothing automatically "escalatory" in this aim. A political decision to stop hostilities can still be made; it is not victory itself that is vital, but the *idea* of victory as the integrating concept at the level of tactical operations. This decision might also help to avoid the kind of civilian adventurism that got us into the Vietnam war—the misguided belief that one can use incremental pain infliction for the achievement of incremental political goals. A return to an understanding of the rational use of local force is the best hope for achieving genuine arms control. Such an understanding would assume that (1) even local war is not to be entered into lightly, and (2) if it is entered into, we must be prepared to win locally.

Second, it is essential that we sever in our policy thinking the mythical, automatic link between failure to reach a diplomatic settlement and instability in the nuclear arms balance. If we are to be effective negotiators, we must be able to sit down at the negotiating table and get up without a settlement without violating our own strategic doctrine.

Finally, we must sever in our policy thinking and in the public mind the mythical, automatic link between the capability to defend ourselves and the paralyzing specter of accidental all-out nuclear war. The international instability that is beginning to follow from Western vulnerability to Soviet strategic forces is sufficient testimony to the bankruptcy of the theory that stability lies in never confronting our adversaries and in never demonstrating the political resolve to defend ourselves. In fact, demonstration of the political resolve to defend ourselves is the best hope of avoiding war.

These measures might help dissolve or disassemble arms control as a comprehensive security policy—a policy that leads toward gradual accommodation up to a point either of great instability or of surrender. They would allow negotiations with the Soviet Union on genuine arms reductions to take place within the context of a stable balance of power. Finally, they would remind us that a technical solution to avoid war can never replace a political solution to achieve peace, and that a balance of power has always been the closest approximation to justice achievable in the international realm.

1982

## Notes

1. "Deterring war is the only sure way to deter use of nuclear weapons." Bernard Brodie, *War and Politics* (New York: Macmillan, 1973), 404.

2. "Military strategy can no longer be thought of . . . as the science of military victory." Thomas Schelling, *Arms and Influence* (New Haven, Conn.: Yale University Press, 1966), 34. "Thus far the chief purpose must be to avert them. It can have almost no other useful purpose." Bernard Brodie in 1946, proudly reaffirmed in *War and Politics*, 377.

3. See, in general, the books, articles, and speeches of, *inter alia*, Bernard Brodie, Thomas Schelling, Robert McNamara, Cyrus Vance, and McGeorge Bundy.

4. "The freeze proposal articulates grave reservations many people have about Ronald Reagan. It will be in his continuing political interest to allay these fears and sound like a peace president, whatever his own instincts and preferences." Michael Barone, "The Political Fallout," *The Washington Post*, 27 April 1982, p. 19.

5. This development is apparent in the differences between the 1962 and 1976 versions of U.S. Army tactical operations doctrine as stated in FM 100–5. Although the new manual pays lip service to the idea of victory, the exposition, unlike that of the 1962 version, is not directed and integrated by that idea but around the problems of targeting with new, fast accurate weapons.

6. Those "military sociologists" interested in accounting for problems in retention of serious officers and noncommissioned officers might address this fundamental dilemma rather than simply concentrating on its effects.

7. The first volume of Henry Kissinger's memoirs provides an interesting

account of this process during the Vietnam war. *White House Years* (Boston: Little Brown and Co., 1979), parts 3 and 4.

8. See the article "Nuclear Weapons and the Atlantic Alliance" by McGeorge Bundy, George Kennan, Robert McNamara, and Gerard Smith in *Foreign Affairs* (Spring 1982): 761–62.

9. The U.S. Air Force has had to deal with its own version of this problem—the requirement in the logic of arms control to target enemy cities with nuclear weapons rather than to target enemy missiles.

10. For a classic exposition of this view, see Schelling, *Arms and Influence*.

# 6
# Accidental Nuclear War and Deterrence: The Two-Edged Sword

## Introduction

The United States finds itself now in the need and mood to conduct an effective foreign policy against an adversary still bent on revolutionizing the world balance of power established at Yalta in 1945. Yet we seem puzzled as to how our intentions might be expressed in actions as our citizens and allies remain divided over appropriate measures for dealing with a recognized Soviet military buildup and the problems of revolutionary warfare in our own hemisphere and elsewhere.

To conduct an effective foreign policy, we need to know what we are capable of, and what we want to do. Major parts of our capabilities, in turn, are dependent on our system of government, the disposition of our citizens, and our military and weapons policies and their effects. The three essays that follow attempt to show that the United States has suffered from a paralysis of its foreign policy capabilities owing to the evolution of a ruling paradigm of thought on national security that has set the horizons and defined the outline of our military (and diplomatic) policies since the Kennedy administration. I call this paradigm, the "crisis management model for security in the nuclear age," and attempt in this book to make explicit its assumptions and implications.

This essay, "Accidental Nuclear War and Deterrence," lays out the postulates of this model or paradigm and attempts to show its explanatory power in accounting for our behavior in the Cuban missile crisis, the Vietnam war, our nuclear weapons policies, and arms negotiations with the Soviet Union. Special attention is paid to the model's fundamental contradiction—the attempt to base deterrence on *both* the dangers *and* vulnerabilities of accidental nuclear war—and its divisive effects on our external policies. The second essay, "Armed Force and Republican Government," explores another of the failings of the crisis management model, the attempt to exclude the majority of citizens from participation in the esoteric subject of deterrence policy, and the intent to ground security in paramilitary operations under the nuclear umbrella. The third related essay, "Armed Force and Political Liberty," examines yet another of the model's failings, the attempt to substitute the punitive or retaliatory use of *conventional* armed force (at the nuclear level we have in fact relied upon the deterrent dangers of preemptive or accidental escalation) as a basis for the maintenance of political authority and liberty.

The diversity in these three essays reflects the thrust of the recommendations—to bring the majority of the American middle class back into deliberation about, and provision of, the common defense as the basis for continued and stable nuclear deterrence, and deterrence of Soviet military aggression. The success of the recommendations may be told in the ability to get two types of readers to read *all three* pieces. The first employs technical military and crisis management terms to aid in the development of a political point—the long term impossibility of grounding national security in policies of magnified vulnerability, against an unaccommodating adversary. The second and third take as their points of departure the existence and failings of the crisis management model, and explore their dangers for political liberty and republican government. Foreign policy specialists, military professionals, and defense analysts are invited to begin with the first piece, and if there is curiosity to go further, to proceed to the third and then second. Students of politics and political theory are invited to begin with the center piece, and move to the third and then first, if interest is maintained.

## The Dilemma

For about two decades, or roughly since John Kennedy's March 1961 Congressional Defense Budget Message, the United States has ostensibly based its security upon a strategy of credible threats and capabilities for controlled and graduated retaliation to deter and compel actions of adversaries.[1] As is now well known, such a policy of flexible retaliation after the fact is at odds with a policy of defense, per se, and even at odds with a policy of deterrence through the capability for defending against attack ("if you would have peace, prepare for war"). Defense connotes warding off and preserving oneself in the face of attack, or imminent attack; deterrence based on defense connotes preventing the outbreak of hostilities through perception of the capability to limit damage to oneself, including the intent to disarm and punish the enemy. These alternatives have been viewed since Bernard Brodie's *The Absolute Weapon* as either obsolete or too destabilizing to provide an acceptable basis for security policy in an age of multilaterally deployed nuclear weapons.

I attempt to demonstrate here that, in fact, our real security policy of the past two decades has not been primarily the threat of assured, unacceptable retaliation to deter and compel opponents, but (whether always consciously or not) the unilateral attempt to attain international "crisis stability" by controlling both our opponents and our own population and military forces through manipuplation of the horrors of uncontrollable or accidental escalation into mutually devastating spasm nuclear war. This has meant among other things retention of an *ambiguous* counterforce capability—itself the outcome of tradeoffs between hawks and doves—to make plausible the deterrent pressures of accidental or preemptive escalation, combined oddly with measures to make ourselves increasingly vulnerable to nuclear war even by accident. Over time, this is proving to be a very unsound policy that threatens to undermine the basis for continued deterrence by undermining political and military cohesion and resolve among those countries that depend on it for their security, while conveying conflicting signals to opponents. As I shall try to show, this policy can no longer provide a viable basis for continued deterrence, because it is *now* the United States that can least (in the face of its own political divisions and military vulnerabilities vis-à-vis much strengthened Soviet military capabilities) tolerate an increasing probability of accidental nuclear war. A new basis for deterrence is necessary, and to achieve it we must think through carefully how the old basis worked at all political and operational levels.

The policy of "stabilizing conflict" through manipulation of the psychological and technological pressures toward and away from[2] accidental and uncontrollable escalation is implied in the assertion that war is no longer politically acceptable because nuclear war would result in mutual devastation. What government could rationally accept such an outcome? Therefore, if nuclear war comes, it must definitionally be the result of an accident, for example, a breakdown (technical, political/military, or a combination) in communications leading to mounting pressures to preempt, either as escalation from limited operations or as a surprise first strike. A policy of manipulation of apparent escalation risks to deter and compel at multiple levels has even been made explicit by formal academic theorists of considerable influence in the defense department, for instance Professor Thomas Schelling of Harvard University, former advisor to former Secretary of Defense McNamara. Or, to go back even further, perhaps the genesis of this policy can be found in what former Secretary of State Dulles seems to have had in mind by the expression "brinkmanship," although to be sure when he spoke the United States had overwhelming nuclear superiority and was in a military position to follow through on such a policy.

Yet I am suggesting more than that the specter of accidental war has always been implied as the real deterrent in the model of assured devastation (who but the naive have ever believed in deliberate, massive, punitive nuclear retaliation after the fact?), or that manipulation of its dangers has been simply one of the techniques available to crisis managers of the "delicate balance of terror." I am suggesting, rather, that not only has the specter of accidental war and its horrors always been logically implicit as the real deterrent in the policy of mutual assured destruction, but that it has in fact served as the basis for our national security policy for the past two decades. (The present administration appears to want to take a different line, but has been unable to accomplish much yet, owing partially to the residual effects of two decades of this policy on the American people.) The effects of this policy are evident in the conduct of our foreign policy during this period and, I will try to show, help greatly to explain our handling of the Cuban missile crisis (when the policy was formulated in practice), the conduct and outcome of the Vietnam war, the current composition of our defense forces and weapons systems (most of which were set in the 1960s under Secretary McNamara), our urgency in negotiations to limit the spread and numbers of nuclear weapons, and the declining usefulness of our worldwide system of defense alliances to contain Soviet expansionism in its various forms.

A policy of reliance upon manipulation of the apparent risks of accidental escalation as the lynchpin of our national security involves both operational and political errors. If I am able to show that the policy has also been the basis for the "new science of crisis management" developed by academic theorists and civilian analysts over the past two decades, then presumably parts of this "new science" will also be undermined by this analysis (especially the explicit claim that it can do service as an alternative to the art of defense, rather than simply complement it). As it happens, however, its own political and military errors along with some help from the Soviet Union are already undermining it, and one can only help to show how, why, and where this is occurring with a view toward constructive changes.

Reliance upon the dangers of accidental nuclear war as the primary basis for deterrence and management of our national interests throughout the world involves a fundamental, political contradiction that is being exacerbated over time. The specter of accidental nuclear war, as it emerged in conjunction with the evolving concept of mutual assured destruction, was expected to perform two incompatible tasks: as an unbearable threat, to induce arms control as well as political and military restraint in all concerned and, in so doing, to minimize or eliminate itself as a threat. This dual aim has forced American crisis managers into the contradictory attempt to generate pressure to minimize or correct the conditions contributing to the dangers of accidental nuclear war and thus give stability to the nuclear arms balance, while simultaneously generating the psychological and practical conditions to make the dangers of accidental nuclear war unbearable as a means to deter and limit aggression at all levels. Additionally, the prospective horrors of accidental nuclear war were to keep both the Soviets and the American people restrained, and supportive of arms control programs and crisis management techniques as the only alternative to all-out nuclear war.[3]

In the absence of full Soviet cooperation in this effort, the long-term effect of this fundamental political error, which blurs the distinction between internal and external policy by seeking to ground international security upon the inability of individual governments to protect their citizens, has been to project normal domestic divisions that historically have stopped at the waters edge behind the goal of the common defense, into the realm of foreign and defense policy. As this division leads to lack of success in external policy toward the Soviet Union and other Marxist-Leninist regimes and raises doubts among our friends as to what our policies really are or can be, the effects can be expected further to rigidify the domestic divisions already making for a divided foreign policy, and so on cyclically, leading to further deterioration in the authority and credibility of the United States government both at home and abroad.

In addition to this political error in grounding our national security ultimately upon the dangers and horrors of accidental nuclear war as the pivot of deterrence, there have been involved as well operational errors, evident in both our military and diplomatic activities. As the Vietnam war made clear, cultivation, both in the public mind and in policy models, of the "automatic links" between any use of conventional armed force and the specter of accidental nuclear war has made it difficult to act decisively with armed force locally, or to negotiate seriously about what is gained in military operations, since military or diplomatic confrontation might lead, on this view, further along the putative chain of events ending in all-out, accidental nuclear war. But as if this were not enough, this policy by the effects of its own logic leads in a developing crisis to increased mutual pressures to strike preemptively since essentially all our protective strategic military resources are placed in offensive "retaliatory" weapons, intended during our period of ICBM superiority in the 1960s to give weight to the threat of uncontrollable escalation into accidental war.

If we are to find our way to "weapons stability" and thus to international stability in the nuclear age, it will be necessary to achieve political stability and cohesion over security issues in the American body politic and the Western alliance as the basis for these other stabilities. Deterrence, if it is to last beyond this generation, must be grounded in political life, not in the futile attempt to deal with the stability of the weapons balance as a technological problem, insulated from political reasoning and developments. This will entail an analysis of the political and strategic implications of a national security policy based for two decades upon the dangers of assured mutual destruction through accidental nuclear war, in order to ascertain which parts of the current policy must be retained, and how they may be coherently integrated into the attempt to provide for military stability in a politically grounded policy of deterrence and defense. Even operationally, this will prove to be a sounder and more enduring basis for deterrence than primary reliance upon a technical model for assured mutual destruction following upon a putative process of accidental escalation, itself the result of actions taken either to gain or deny a critical military or political advantage in a confrontation. In brief, assured destruction is not simply a physical fact of life deterring the use of armed force for political ends in the thermonuclear age. How we think and react to the existence of nuclear weapons in our national security policies has political and military effects over the long-term with implications for political stability and continued deterrence, which American crisis managers (in contrast to Marxist-Leninist elites) at their own peril seem not yet to have begun to address seriously.

## The Model

In the early years following World War II, two distinct ideas were put forth for the control of nuclear weapons by means putatively independent of political and military processes and reasoning. The first was that nuclear atomic weapons could not be effectively defended against; thus, their operational use would lead to widespread devastation and, if responded to in kind, would result in mutual devastation. The second idea was that the way to deter both aggression and possible use of such weapons was through assurance of punitive retaliation including the possible defensive use of atomic weapons in the event of attack, thus denying to the aggressor the benefits of his aggression.[4] Already present in these postulates was the presupposition that nuclear (atomic) war would have to begin by accident or miscalculation, because in the event of aggression the consequences of initiating the use of nuclear weapons either by attacker or defender would be assured devastation through retaliation in kind greater than any possible gain deriving from their use, and no government could rationally choose that. Nevertheless, it took another decade, some further weapons developments, and some theorizing about those developments, to make accidental nuclear war the pivot of deterrence—at least for the initiated.

By about the end of the 1950s, after the Soviet Union acquired atomic weapons, and then the United States and the Soviet Union acquired thermonuclear weapons and missiles to deliver them quickly to targets in other continents, the view was expressed in both Congressional hearings and theoretical literature, that deterrence of nuclear attack was not assured since retaliation could not be assured if both sides had thermonuclear weapons that could be used decisively in a surprise attack to disarm the opponent's missiles. (On the contrary, "rationally" in a bipolar world in which both sides were armed with nuclear weapons, the existence of a vulnerable, decisive strike capability was a provocation for the opponent to strike first.) It was at this point that there began to crystallize in U.S. circles the recognition that deterrence could not be allowed to rest upon a delicate balance of terror,[5] but that the balance must be stabilized by maintenance on both sides of complex weapons configurations that assured devastating retaliation ("finite deterrence"), yet did not unambiguously threaten a preventive, disarming first strike. Concurrently, there was also the unspoken recognition that it was the presumed delicacy or fragility of the "balance of terror" that gave weight and credibility to the apolitical arguments of the assured destruction school, and that might serve to deter all rapid military escalation through the genuine dangers of accidental preemptive escalation.

The idea of accidental war now became the explicit villain (the very idea of preventing accidents falling within the technical rather than the political domain). Accidental war had by this time two meanings, one obvious and one deeper. In its explicit meaning, the expression referred to the outbreak of nuclear war through mechanical failure, "psychological aberration," communications breakdowns, or miscalculation (for example, an unnecessary preemptive strike). Extending the idea of miscalculation, it could also mean more deeply that the outbreak of nuclear war between the United States and the Soviet Union would definitionally be an accident, because the more enlightened or rational adversary would opt out of confrontation (so long as communication channels remained open and escalation did not occur too rapidly) before accepting the alternative of assured destruction.[6]

To politically minded individuals and the uniformed military, this would have sounded like a plan for surrender if made explicit. But the advocates of this view, from atomic scientists to game theorists, had already come to the conclusion that strategic surrender was an obsolete political concept relevant perhaps to conflict between fixed, opposing political entities like sovereign states, but not to mutually enlightened partners of somewhat fluid identity engaged in a joint enterprise to make their best deals around the world by invoking the dangers of, and thus averting, their presumed mutual, technological enemy—accidental nuclear war. There began, in almost Orwellian fashion, the construction of an economic game theory and vocabulary of war that would make it difficult for anyone adopting it to find words and concepts to think about or formulate with any precision policies for the political use or threat of armed force, even at conventional force levels. It viewed war as a game of coercive bargaining in which both parties by adopting its logic could recognize themselves to be better off (though not necessarily equally so) by averting war, or terminating it sooner than later. Psychologically, it involved transferal of loyalties from more abiding identities and habits deep in the personality, to an externally visible (and thus presumably controllable) matrix of discrete and presumably quantifiable values constructed to avert war by finding payoffs of some sort to all engaged. Applied with "scientific" arrogance at the level of conventional armed force to an enemy who refused to recognize its logic, this view contributed significantly to our strategic shortcomings in the Vietnam war (a subsequent subject of this essay).

By the mid-1960s, behind the momentum of the McNamara "defense" department and its reading of the Cuban missile crisis of 1962, there crystallized a basic outlook or paradigm (parts of it still unspoken) on the security of the United States that has endured with but slight modification for two decades and that is a fundamental source of our diplomatic and military difficulties today. Its essence is to guarantee political accommodation by holding both military forces and civilian populations hostage to mutually guaranteed, massive, preemptively invoked, "retaliatory" nuclear capabilities. It has proved to be a politically and strategically destabilizing program of "security" grounded upon manipulation of increasingly unacceptable dangers leading to accidental or uncontrollable escalation into nuclear war, although it has presented itself as an overall policy of deterrence of aggression through threat of graduated and flexible retaliation and reprisal. In its essentials, it evolved to encompass the following:[7]

1. If the security of the United States (and the world) were seen to rest simply upon deterring Soviet aggression through threat of retaliation in kind, we would be counting on just another version of the old balance of power, which in the past has not always maintained itself, deterred aggression, and averted war. Nor are the massive casualties of full-scale conventional war as occurred in the world wars, or the sustained casualties of a limited Korean-like war, viewed as any longer acceptable. In the light of modern weapons technology, something more positive than a simply retaliation-in-kind capability and less costly than a balance-of-power conventional military capability would be essential to an effective military policy that could both deter aggression and compel compliance without resort to war.

2. The vast destructive potential of nuclear weapons can be

expected to induce mutual cooperation in weapons system levels and configurations designed to assure to both the Soviet Union and the United States a significant retaliatory capability in the event of (imminent) attack. Further, if measures to protect weapons and populations can be avoided, pressures to raise the destructive level of the assured retaliatory (preemptive and punitive) component can be avoided. In this way, mutual assured destruction becomes the key to avoiding an arms race in ICBMs, or their preemptive use in the event of confrontations, to the mutual advantage of both the Soviet Union and the United States.

3. If mutual destruction of both the Soviet Union and the United States is assured in the event of spasm nuclear war, then the outbreak of such a war must definitionally be an accident or miscalculation, since neither country could rationally be expected to invite assured destruction. Thus, the key to deterring aggression at whatever level is the threat of graduated and flexible retaliation and continued reprisals to punish an aggressor, deny him the benefits of his aggression short of war, and deter him from continued aggression through credible threat of uncontrollable escalation of conflict. But the credibility of such threats depends ultimately upon their linkage with the power of the Soviet Union and the United States, both of which must be expected to act with restraint.

4. But since mutual destruction cannot be automatically assured, we must work at ensuring it by stabilizing the "delicate balance of terror." Stabilization ultimately involves proper cultivation of the conditions and pressures leading to and away from accidental nuclear war, rather than resting upon attempts to maintain diplomatic and operational initiative through threats of preemptive and punitive retaliation. (In fact, an ambiguous counterforce capability is desirable to give weight to the war-deterring threat of uncontrollable preemptive escalation, since the threat of punitive retaliation on populations after the fact lacks both spontaneity and credibility.) Graduated retaliatory capabilities exist not to threaten opponents, *but to force them to restrain themselves* in the face of the credible specter of accidental or uncontrollable escalation of preemptive and punitive measures. Thus, political and military restraint will always be a consequence of one's own initiative, rather than an unavoidable option forced upon one by the opposing side. Like it or not, we are all now partners in a joint enterprise rather than opposing political entities, because either superpower can unilaterally destroy the

other if it is willing to accept its own destruction as well, re-
*gardless of steps the other might take to escape this fate.*

5. The real function of crisis managers of "the balance of
terror," then, is to work to restrain the Soviets and other potential
"destabilizers" by using the threat of gradual but escalating reprisals to call up in their own minds the vision of even more pain
and the possibility of uncontrollable escalation into accidental
nuclear war; simultaneously, the domestic task of crisis managers is to heighten perceived dangers of accidental nuclear war
among the American people and military forces, in order to
contain sentiments to confront or use armed forces decisively to
disarm or defeat. Measures to control the civilian population
include media and public discussion of the dangers of escalation
and the horrors of nuclear war, as well as efforts to assure the
absence of serious civil defense or missile defense preparations
that might qualify the status of citizens as hostages to accidental
nuclear war. Measures to control the uniformed military's attempt to perform their traditional function by maintaining tactical initiative and continuity of operations toward a military end
include, first, gradual substitution in official literature of an
economic vocabulary of armed force solely as a means to inflict
punitive reprisals, and containing no concepts for the decisive
use of force for military and political goals, at any operational
level; second, bureaucratic reorganization to exclude military
leadership from serious operational decision making, direct control over their own forces, or direct access to the chief executive;
and third, bureaucratic devices to inhibit decisive military action, primarily through requirement to justify on grounds of cost-
effectiveness each increment of additional resources requested.
The military forces of allies must be constrained as well from the
decisive and defensive use of force against major enemies or their
proxies, although the method of control will vary from major
allies who must be dealt with by diplomatic assertion (e.g.,
Israel) to minor allies who are susceptible to integration into our
own operational chain of command (e.g., South Vietnam).

6. The specter of accidental nuclear war can thus serve as a
two-edged sword to be wielded from a putatively apolitical,
pivotal position by crisis managers of "the delicate balance of
terror," against either their own populations and military forces
(or those of their allies), or against those of opponents and enemies in order to eliminate the possibility of not only nuclear
war, but eventually all armed aggression. In time, a class of
enlightened crisis managers should arise in the Soviet Union and

begin to cooperate against our presumed common, technological enemy—accidental nuclear war; until that occurs, conflict can be stabilized by shifting the pivotal point further into the home court of the more accommodating player.

## The Model vs. the Conduct of Military Operations

Since this policy model was used in Vietnam to direct the overall conduct of fighting with conventional armed force as a bargaining process (i.e., "infliction of punitive reprisals"), it is instructive as part of its elaboration to contrast it with the traditional principles for the conduct of successful military operations. (This contrast also has ramifications for the organization of the Department of Defense. What is the subject matter of that department? Crisis management? The conduct of military operations? Or both? And who, civilian appointees or professional military, should be in charge of which?)

For sake of exposition, the major differences have been organized into six categories which mirror the fluidity of actual practice by overlapping somewhat.[8]

1. The *aim* of military operations has been to preserve oneself and contain violence by defeating or disarming enemy forces as steps on the way to achieving political goals. Even in so-called wars of attrition, the aim has been to inflict destruction in a sustained manner sufficient to induce physical and moral *shock* in enemy forces and their leadership in order to end the fighting and generate psychological and political pliability at the negotiating table.

By contrast, the *aim* of the new science of crisis management is to contain violence and coerce opponents *through rational calculation* to a political settlement of near mutual advantage through the threat of graduated (intermittent) punitive reprisals against a backdrop of the possibility of uncontrollable escalation to larger war.

2. The basic principles of successful military operations demand that forces preempt the initiative even when on the strategic or tactical defensive (a point well understood by communist strategists like Mao and Giap); act decisively and maintain continuity of operations; conceal plans from the enemy; and isolate the battle area to prevent enemy resupply, rescue, or undesired escape.

By contrast, the operational principles of crisis management demand relinquishing the military initiative in order to avert preemptive attack presumably by either side (while magnifying the deterrent appearance of uncontrollability); acting only in reaction to punish aggressors and "demonstrate resolve"; acting slowly and intermittently in order to be capable of stopping at any time; and making general plans known to the enemy beforehand in order to permit "coercive bargaining" (i.e., acting preemptively only in the realm of speech).

3. The conduct of successful military operations for the achievement of political goals requires attainment of military superiority within the theater of operations to reduce or eliminate fighting and permit the restoration of political control.

By contrast, the new science of crisis management seeks only sufficient military results to sustain the credible threat of retaliation and possible escalation to larger punitive operations as bargaining techniques.

4. The conduct of successful military operations requires the employment of force decisively to defeat enemy military forces when possible; even in attrition warfare, its objective is to use the destructive effects of firepower to induce sustained physical, psychological, and systemic (political) shock in the enemy.

By contrast, the new science of crisis management requires the threat of graduated, intermittent pain infliction to induce desired *calculations* in minds of enemy leaders about the relative mutual advantages to bargaining; it requires the avoidance of shock in enemy leadership since the results might be uncontrollable and irrational. (The aim is to create the illusion of resolve to escalate the level of damage—not the intensity of fighting to win—up to a point of potential uncontrollability, while consolidating real control over the situation through accommodation of objectives.)

5. The conduct of successful military operations requires control by military leadership over the details of fluid, armed operations, directed toward support of goals of political leadership (again, well understood by revolutionary, Marxist-Leninist movements).

By contrast, the new science of crisis management requires detailed direction by civilian crisis managers of armed operations, *in the name of political control*. This is required since, on this view, the real activity occurring is coercive bargaining, not military operations, and crisis managers have more expertise at this activity than military leaders who might try to control the outcome of armed conflict by attempting to preempt the initiative rather than seek mutually beneficial bargaining through intermittent punitive reprisals.

6. In general, the conduct of military operations views armed conflict as a step on the way to a desired political condition following (or simultaneous with) physical or psychological defeat of enemy forces.

By contrast, the new science of crisis management conceives of armed operations as discrete exercises in targeting and destruction to induce enemy leadership to bargain through rational calculation of the relative advantages of options open to them.

To summarize, the difference between these two activities, housed in the same Department of "Defense," involves both conflicting aims and, in turn, methods. Crisis management attempts to contain violence by offering enemy leadership opportunities and incentives to restrain its own military forces, that is, through devices to create the illusion of our resolve to continue to escalate the level of retaliation while reducing our own military effectiveness—for example, by relinquishing the military initiative or increasing the vulnerability of our own population. If the enemy leadership refuses to be either deterred or coopted, and remains in political consolidation with its own forces and population, crisis management in the name of "limited war" becomes a program for our own political defeat or subordination, as occurred in Vietnam, and is now in danger of occurring vis-à-vis the Soviet Union worldwide. Reckoning upon the time-proven likelihood of enemy cohesion in the face of threat, the conduct of military operations, by contrast, attempts to contain violence primarily by developing capabilities and methods for limiting damage to itself and skillfully disarming or controlling enemy forces. If, in the event, diplomatic or intelligence efforts are able to coopt enemy leadership or population, so much the better; but this has not been counted on historically as the primary basis for security, especially that of a country with a popularly elected government like the United States.

## The Model, the Cuban Missile Crisis, and the Vietnam War

I have suggested thus far that in the name of a "strategy of flexible response" (designed in part to preserve flexibility or latitude to avoid the kind of rapid escalation that characterized the outbreak of World War I) there evolved a policy model for handling all armed conflict and potential armed conflict as a form of crisis management both to use and minimize the dangers of uncontrollable escalation into larger conflict and possibly nuclear war. The operating mechanism in the model was, in the interest of crisis and weapons stability, to offer adversary leadership the opportunity to manage their population in the fashion that our own crisis management limited shifts of relative advantage in the balance of power. This was done by developing capabilities for (and in Vietnam actually taking) incremental, retaliatory measures to create the illusion of resolve to escalate gradually the level of retaliation in the expectation that, first, adversary leadership would be constrained by the illusory threat of escalation and be compelled to conform to our political goals *(best outcome)*; second, if enemy leadership saw through the threat or ignored it, they should at least see that we were also using the real and illusory dangers of uncontrollable escalation of conflict to control and limit our own population and military forces, and thus might do the same to theirs (i.e., accept the crisis management model); third, even if adversary leadership refused to cooperate in limiting conflict in this fashion and prepared for or attempted decisive military action, escalation of conflict would have at least been controlled by our own pliability, albeit at the expense of some of our political and military interests. This would still be *a better of undesirable outcomes* than the fourth or *worst possibility* in the model—both sides threatening or attempting to defend their interests through decisive military action, with the real possibility of uncontrollable escalation of conflict.

This policy model began to evolve in the Kennedy administration during the "Cuban missile crisis" of 1962 when the precepts of formal theorists of "stable conflict" like T. C. Schelling were given concrete meanings by President Kennedy's special executive committee and by Secretary of Defense McNamara and his deputies. It is reported that Secretary McNamara began the special committee discussions with a proposal that would have defused the crisis immediately by suggesting that "a missile is a missile" and that we accept the Soviet missiles in Cuba without creating an incident.[9] Although this temporary solution might prove politically acceptable in the United States now after two decades of this model's influence on attitudes and military capabilities, it was not a politically acceptable solution in 1962. After rejecting as well the military proposal for surgical air strikes to destroy the intermediate-range nuclear missiles already in Cuba before they could be assembled, President Kennedy and his special executive committee opted for a naval blockade ("quarantine") to prevent further increase in the number of Soviet missiles in Cuba. Although this measure provided the Soviets with the opportunity to rush to assemble the missiles already in Cuba, it did satisfy the crisis management requirement for beginning with low-level retaliation, and it did relinquish the burden of the next initiative to the Soviets. This is the critical point in the analysis of this crisis and the model. The aim was to continue to place on the enemy or adversary the onus of initiating a chain of events necessary to sustain his political-military position, but which might lead to uncontrollable escalation. America's (then) vastly superior "deterrent forces" would be called into play only accidentally.

Thus, the sequence of events became critical for Kennedy after the Soviets and Cubans shot down a U.S. reconnaissance aircraft and continued in the face of warnings to shoot at others as they tried to monitor assembly of the missiles in Cuba. Kennedy realized that if another U.S. plane were brought down, it was the United States that would be forced into initiating military escalation. Thus, he quickly took steps to force the blockade issue (where the Soviets would be compelled into taking the initiative), while offering them privately a way out of the confrontation—the promise not to invade Cuba and some sort of deal to remove U.S. intermediate range missiles in Turkey and Italy (eventually removed from Germany as well), in return for cessation of their attempt to put intermediate-range missiles in Cuba.

Soviet compliance with the proposal led to several unwarranted conclusions in the Kennedy administration that made the crisis management model appear more effective than it really was. It was assumed in some vague way that the outcome was a U.S. victory because the Soviets backed down from placing intermediate-range missiles in Cuba in exchange for U.S. abandonment of the Monroe Doctrine (the basis of our Caribbean policy since 1823) not to permit the introduction of a new, foreign military presence in this hemisphere, and the promise to remove U.S. intermeidate-range missiles in Europe. Additionally, it was also seen as a victory because the Soviets appeared to have accepted the logic of the crisis management model of maneuvering for limited gains while avoiding uncontrollable escalation into nuclear war. (If the Soviets had really understood the logic of the model as well as they apparently do now, to judge by their successes in using it against us, they would have known how remote the possibility that President Kennedy would ever have allowed U.S. conventional forces to invade Cuba.)

Yet there was little basis for our own assumptions.[10] The Soviets appear to have backed down when they did because they had already gained quite a bit, and because the United States had vast nuclear and regional, conventional military superiority at that time and place. Like the fantasies of a rich kid that are tolerated because, when all is said and done, he really does have the money to do what he wants, U.S. intellectual fantasies in this matter were tolerated because we really did have the military capability to enforce our will in the Caribbean at that time (under the deterrent umbrella of a vastly superior nuclear force). What we really accomplished in this nominal U.S. crisis management victory was to make unnecessary concessions in a confrontation we would have simply dominated; to misread the reasons for the limited success we did achieve; and to set the stage for the misguided application of the same crisis management bargaining techniques of incremental retaliation to call up the specter of accidental war, in another corner of the world, against a different enemy, in a much different political setting, and where our resolve and capabilities were more ambiguous. Additionally, the precedent was set for detailed, civilian crisis manager control directly over the details of military operations—for example, issuance of navigational instructions minute by minute or specification of aircraft altitudes—as a method of "stabilizing conflict" in a crisis.

Applied and further developed under the misnomer of "limited war" in Vietnam, this model of crisis management demonstrated through its successive failures its failings when applied at the level of conventional armed force operations against Marxist-Leninist militia, regional and main force units, to coerce an already long-committed enemy leadership into political accommodation. The model, as a set of (partially unspoken) assumptions defining the horizons within which we operated, helps to explain so many otherwise puzzling developments in a ten-year conflict in which U.S. military forces lost no major battle, yet in which our government was unable to attain our major political goal—preservation of the government of South Vietnam in the face of an increasingly overt North Vietnamese invasion.

To begin with, the scientific arrogance of the model and its formulators can explain our failure to investigate in depth the nature of the enemy, from their long history of determined resistance to non-Vietnamese control to the fact that, by the time we began bombing reprisals in 1965, the North Vietnamese military effort in the South had been continuously under way since 1959; the North Vietnamese Politburo leadership that had instigated it against internal opposition could hardly afford to turn back, especially in the face of only incrementally applied pressures.[11] Yet the model and its makers, operating on the modern rationalist canon of the universal applicability of the scientific method, calculated in some vague way that it should work against anybody, anywhere, and certainly against a "minor" Asian people after it appeared to have worked against the Soviets in Cuba.

The model also helps to explain the emphasis upon detailed civilian crisis manager control over the operational aspects of the war—for example, planning for the course of the war, setting quantitative standards for measuring *military* success such as the body count, parceling out bombing authorization a few days at a time, even issuing technical directives about altitude levels and models of cameras to be used in surveillance. If the activity we were really engaged in was management of punitive reprisals to stabilize conflict until desired outcomes could be attained in negotiations, rather than the conduct of military operations to disarm the enemy or induce pliability through shock effect of sustained firepower, then who was the more qualified to perform this task? Arguably, civilian crisis managers! Leaving the real conduct of major operations in military hand risked genuine escalation of conflict, on this view, through application of military principles to attain military victory or at least induce sustained shock and bewilderment as a prelude to a political settlement. (Even the "search and destroy" missions and the Cambodian "incursion" were only brief expressions of constrained military initiative to hold down our own casualties in the face of an aggressive enemy, not part of a plan to defeat or decisively control enemy forces.) Unfortunately, this civilian takeover violated a supreme rule of any practical endeavor—it severed the link between responsibility for execution and responsibility for success.

The model can also explain puzzles in the actual conduct of the war. The requirements to begin reprisals slowly and intermittently and to relinquish the military initiative in order to contain one's own military reactions to developing circumstances, while seeking to create the illusion of inexorable escalation in the level of retaliation as inducements to bargaining, go a long way in explaining a wide variety of questions that have been raised about the conduct of the war. These requirements of the model explain, for example, why there was no single military commander responsible for a specific military goal in both North and South Vietnam; they explain why the "air war"[12] in the North to punish the enemy and the ground war in the South to stabilize the South Vietnamese government were coordinated only insofar as was necessary to keep the South Vietnamese government from collapsing at any moment, not sufficiently to attempt final military victory over North Vietnamese and Viet Cong forces; they explain why there was no really serious attempt to isolate the ground battle area in South Vietnam (preparatory to decisive military action) by critical and sustained interdiction of transfer points (harbors, depots, rail junctions) along the supply route through which moved enemy personnel, armor, and artillery from North to South, often via Cambodia and Laos; they explain why U.S. ground forces were *permitted* to develop what General Westmoreland called a "fire-base psychosis"[13] in which they began to lose the skills and organization to engage and control enemy forces through decisive fire and maneuver, and came to rely upon firepower for their primary offensive capability (thus supporting the crisis management model's refusal to distinguish between escalation of destruction and escalation in the intensity of skillful operations to control the enemy); and they explain U.S. willingness (complicity?) to identify the problem in the South as "insurgency" rather than as a covert invasion from the North, because the former problem would not require decisive military action whereas the latter arguably would and because additionally, identification of a Northern invasion might have mobilized the American people behind the war, a development not conducive to "stabilized conflict."

Finally, the illusory expectation in the apolitical crisis management model that there would be an automatic leap from the effects of technology (i.e., destruction) to desired outcomes at the negotiating table explains in part the failure to recognize the critical link between the preemptive use of force and the structuring of political authority in South Vietnam. The connection *between* the (politically) defensive use of force *and* authority, a lesson we still understood during the Korean war when we supported the absolute authority of the South Korean government under Syngman Rhee,[14] was also well understood by the Vietnamese communists who, while leaving the conduct of fluid military operations in the hands of military commanders, always made these operations conform to the goals of political cadres, even at the local level. Yet, ironically, in the name of "political control of the war" (i.e., top-level civilian control of the details of armed operations), top-level management in the Pentagon assumed in some vague way that there would be automatic leaps *from* technological effects *to* formally negotiated outcomes *without* an interlocking chain of political and military authority to make it happen. Their major task appeared to them as the requirement to contain military escalation while creating the illusion that, in the absence of political accommodation, it might become uncontrollable. Yet this blindness to the need for, and workings of, the mechanisms of political control is one of the most worrisome developments in the model of crisis management of the dangers of uncontrollable escalation, a subject of subsequent essays in this book.

Interestingly enough, however, crisis managers like Secretary McNamara and his deputies understood well enough the mechanisms of bureaucratic control that do not rely directly upon the threat or use of armed force. This is evident in their success in imposing their model of crisis management upon the uniformed military within the Department of Defense, and in getting it accepted by large numbers of Americans (who still have not faced up to its long-range implications). Relying upon the already existent authority of Section 101(j) of the 1958 revisions to the National Security Act, which makes all combatant commands responsible to the Secretary of Defense for military missions assigned them by the Secretary of Defense, Mr. McNamara and his deputies (whether always consciously or not) began the rearrangement of procedures, doctrine, and vocabulary to substitute subtly and gradually the activity of crisis management for the art of defense.[15] Again, if our national security is to be based upon manipulation of the readily apparent dangers of accidental escalation, then this would seem a proper and logically consistent development.

Control was exerted over the military profession to incline it to participate in its own mutation into a crisis management security force through three overlapping means. The first was the establishment, as the basis for official approval of military requests, of the language and criteria of crisis management as developed by formal theorists in think tanks and universities, including an economic vocabulary designed to standardize military activity in terms of quantified, cost-efficient options; the second was the increasing exclusion of the uniformed military from high-level strategic decision making and from unhampered control over its own armed operations; the third was the impoundment, as it were, by the Secretary of Defense of his authority and responsibility to generate military missions under the 1958 revisions. These three measures all congealed to constrain and begin mutation of the military services by simultaneously limiting and channeling the conceptual basis for their requests, while tying up their time in preparation of quantified, cost-efficient options or packages for all requests for increased personnel, weapons, material, and so forth. Additionally, this procedure absolved the Secretary of Defense from having to generate military missions or accept responsibility for having formulated them if they failed— he had only to select one option from a package, responsibility for execution of which devolved back upon the military services or the unified commander.

The thrust of the conceptual changes was either to alter the meaning of established military terms (e.g., use of "strategic" and "tactical" to refer to budgeting categories for larger and smaller weapons rather than more and less general operations to attain military goals such as victory); to substitute the language of punitive retaliation for the language of defense (e.g., "to inflict pain on the North Vietnamese,"[16] rather than to defeat or control them); or to reduce the scope of strategic thought through requirement for quantifiable measures of success (e.g., the body count, the number of villages "pacified," projected dollar/destruction ratios, etc.). Needless to say, the greatest friction occurred with the army, which operates on land where political arrangements and settlements transpire and whose mission is the least quantifiable and the most closely linked to the maintenance of political authority. There was less friction with the air force, the most technological service and the one most able to quantify measures of success for its missions (e.g., number and size of bombs dropped), and the service whose theories of strategic bombing provided the intellectual seedbed for the whole deterrence theory of mutual assured destruction after World War II. The navy was somewhat inbetween, but has seen those of its capabilities most associated with military missions (e.g., sea control and ability to transport troops and material) the least promoted. Still, even the army was sufficiently coopted to its own mutation into a crisis management security force under the rubrics of "paramilitary operations" and "counterinsurgency" that the now notorious 1976 version of its basic tactical doctrine (FM100-5) essentially codified the view of armed operations as a series of exercises in targeting to stabilize conflict rather than seriously attempt to disarm or physically and psychologically control enemy forces. (Nor is it clear that these problems have been overcome by the present administration. Probably the most important question for continued deterrence of Soviet aggression throughout the world is whether the military services of the United States are any longer *structured* to conduct decisive military operations.)[17]

Ironically, it seems that the U.S. officer corps may have been the only one in the world capable of this kind of cooperation in the mutation of its own profession owing to its tradition of genuine loyalty and subordination to civilian leadership, and its typically American disinclination to think in broad or long-range political terms. Most British or Western European military leaders would probably have seen better the implications of what was occurring; most non-Western European military leaders would never have felt strong loyalty to civilian leadership; no Leninist regime would have conceived of a plan for voluntary subordination of political and military aims to technological requirements.

## The Model and U.S. Nuclear Weapons Forces and Defenses

The model can explain with the tightest fit the composition of our nuclear weapons forces and defenses up until the Reagan administration. (The military may have close control over the use of weapons; the Congress may have the closest control over the amount of funding for production of the weapons; but it has been civilian Pentagon leadership that exerts the greatest control over the kind of nuclear weapons produced.) The most operative requirement in the crisis management model for the composition of our nuclear forces has been the following: to construct and control nuclear arms in such a way that in a confrontation the pressures to strike preemptively (or take the military initiative) remain credible but minimized, while our vital interests are somehow preserved. In other words, the requirement is to keep credible the deterrent threat of uncontrollable escalation into accidental war, while controlling and eliminating pressures that might make accidental escalation actually occur. Unfortunately, in the absence of cooperation by adversary elites to control their own forces and population similarly, this contradiction in the model becomes a plan for the incremental political, physchological, and military subordination of the side unilaterally adopting it. Still, even unilateral adoption of the plan can work to eliminate pressures to take the military initiative or strike preemptively, if one side makes itself sufficiently vulnerable, psychologically and militarily.

It is the requirement for *mutual* vulnerability of nuclear weapons (partial) and population (complete), *unilaterally* carried out by United States crisis managers over a period of two decades, that both bespeaks the diminution of the threat of accidental war as a credible basis for continued deterrence of Soviet aggression and general war, and that most explains the current shape of our nuclear forces. In the logic of the model, increasing the vulnerability of our weapons and population would presumably have a wide range of effects: first, it would eliminate the need for the Soviets ever to strike at us *quickly*—if neither the weapons nor our population have any protection or evacuation procedures, they can be destroyed at any time, thus leaving open room for a negotiated settlement; second, it would convey to Soviet elites the seriousness of our intentions to rely upon this model as a basis for world security; third, it would increase the real and in turn psychological burden of the danger of even accidental nuclear war weighing upon the now very vulnerable American people; and fourth, it would diminish the likelihood of any subsequent American attempt to construct a nuclear deterrent based upon the capability to defend, since the American people would by now be sufficiently psychologically and physically vulnerable as to be unlikely to vote the political and financial support necessary for such a project, especially if the operative reflexes were generated by public invocations of the specter of accidental nuclear war.

The requirement in the model to keep ourselves relatively vulnerable in order to minimize Soviet pressures to develop an unambiguous, preemptive capability explains best why we have no serious civil defense program, no antiballistic missile program, and a very limited air defense force. It also explains why our least vulnerable weapons, the missiles of the Polaris-Poseidon submarine force, were built with very small warheads (ca. 40 kiloton) and insufficient accuracy to be used against Soviet missiles in a preemptive strike. They were clearly intended as a relatively invulnerable, anti-population/industry second strike to make the specter of accidental war more threatening to the Soviets. The "destabilizing" likelihood that bombers might be sent out to threaten and thus create the appearance of U.S.

military initiative helps to explain why B-1 bomber funding was canceled in 1977 under crisis manager Carter.

The contradictory requirement in the model to keep credible the threat of uncontrollable escalation into accidental war as the basis for deterring war requires a credible response to limited aggression to deter it and provide the basis for coercive diplomacy, and thus the avoidance of war itself through avoidance of confrontation. It helps explain our retention of an ambiguous counterforce capability on the thousand land-based Minuteman II and multiple-warheaded Minuteman II intercontinental ballistic missiles. In order to make credible the deterrent effect of the dangers of accidental war, it is necessary to maintain mutual pressures for damage-limiting, preemptive counterforce strikes against enemy missiles, at least to some degree—otherwise there is little danger of preemptive escalation, since preemptive strikes against civilian populations make little military or moral sense. If there is no longer an at least ambiguous capability for a preemptive counterforce strike, then our invocation of the dangers of uncontrollable escalation carries little deterrent weight ("ambiguous" in order that it can be disguised as a punitive retaliatory force and an arms race in preemptive capabilities avoided). Additionally, placing multiple warheads on the Minuteman III missiles was intended (in addition to being cost-efficient) to give them a limited invulnerability, but one controlled by the initiative of the Soviet Union in a way not possible if the missiles were protected by antimissile missiles. If several warheads were placed on one missile, then the Soviets could be sure we could not afford to leave it in its silo if fired upon, and thus, on this view, would not find it advantageous to resort to threat of military initiative with nuclear weapons.

It was the retention of this ambiguous counterforce capability (Minutemen III had high accuracy but relatively small 170-kiloton warheads; Minutemen II had one larger warhead with less accuracy) that has made the Soviets dubious of our claims about mutual security through assured punitive retaliatory strikes. Perhaps they have never really penetrated to the esoteric aspects of the model of deterrence based ultimately upon invoking the dangers of accidental (i.e., preemptive) escalation. For whatever combination of reasons, including their correct perception that political authority is grounded in part in the perceived ability to provide for the common defense, they developed a counterforce capability in the SS-18 missile. The fact that original implementers of the assured destruction model like Robert McNamara,

McGeorge Bundy, and Cyrus Vance are now opposed to U.S. development of a similar counterforce capability in the MX missile, while making explicit to the American people the dangers of accidental war, suggests that they have shifted to a fallback position, a "less better" of the worse outcomes. It appears that they have concluded that although the specter of accidental war has lost much of its power to deter the Soviet Union, it can at least be used to deter the now (after two decades of the model) very vulnerable American people. Probably it is calculated that U.S.-Soviet relations can be stabilized somewhat in the face of Soviet military aggression and its threat, by unambiguous elimination of a U.S. preemptive capability. Although it is probably also calculated that this will result in some U.S. political and military subordination throughout the world, as long as we have a minimum deterrent we can at least preserve our borders. This may prove to be a political rather than simply a military miscalculation, if, in the face of Soviet military assertion, we begin to elect leadership that sees the only alternative to nuclear war in incremental, unilateral disarmament and accommodation.

## The Model and Arms Control

The expression "arms control" has come to have both public and private meanings in the crisis management paradigm.[18] Publically, as its name implies, it has meant formal and informal agreements to limit the types and numbers of weapons systems being produced. More privately, it has also come to mean reliance upon control over weapons production and deployment as the primary basis for "stabilizing deterrence" while preserving our national interests throughout the world. Stabilized deterrence would presumably be achieved through control over nuclear and conventional arms to eliminate any usable advantage in seizing the military initiative even defensively or striking preemptively, and to control escalation of nuclear conflict should it begin or threaten to begin, through means such as assured retaliatory capabilities, ambiguous preemptive capabilities, permanently vulnerable hostage populations, and organizationally constrained conventional armed forces. Adopted unilaterally by the United States since the Kennedy administration, the model and its contradiction to base deterrence upon the dangers of uncontrollable preemptive escalation while making ourselves more vulnerable to such an accident (e.g., absence of Ballistic

Missile Defense, serious civil defense and air defense) is resulting in our abandonment of the original deterrent basis of the
model—the dangers of accidental war. This occurs as we become,
through our own policies of two decades, the more physically
and psychologically vulnerable party to the dangers of accidental war. The same individuals in the Kennedy and Johnson administration who (perhaps in accommodation to greater military
influence at the time) permitted an ambiguous counterforce capability to be built (the Minutemen III missiles) now oppose its
equivalent in the 1980s (the MX and Pershing II missiles), relying
instead on the "mere existence" of nuclear weapons to deter war
and presumably Soviet aggression as well. That this is a fallback
position—reflecting, were it adopted, a diminution in the U.S.
power and bargaining position vis-à-vis the Soviets—is apparent
in the change it would mean for "arms control."

In the 1960s, the game theory models of the crisis managers
and arms controllers envisioned making the Soviets into a status
quo rather than a revolutionary power by drawing them into
coercive bargaining under the nuclear umbrella for necessarily
small gains throughout the world. The arms controllers apparently intended using our advantage in nuclear weapons in such a
cost-efficient way as to retain initiative by forcing onto the Soviets in any crisis the deterrent burden of initiating the next level of
conflict escalation. (This was to be the operational meaning of
the doctrine of "flexible response.") It should have been apparent
that by beginning unilaterally to halt ICBM production in the
1960s and increase our own vulnerability, we would eventually
forego the ability to control crises in this way. But I believe this
was seen as an educative process for both the American public
(and military forces) and the Soviet leadership, under the tutelage of crisis managers (who had glimpsed and were willing to
gamble on the direction of world historical progress?).[19] Thus,
although the model has been able to some degree to divide and
drain the American people, it does not appear to have had the
same effect on that very *political* group of men running the
Soviet Union, to judge by their nuclear and conventional force
buildup of the past two decades.

The Soviet Union is now beginning to acquire the capabilities
to force onto us the requirement to escalate conflict (or accommodate) in confrontation throughout the world. By developing and
building a full range of land, sea, and air conventional and
nuclear forces, and in combination with the catalyst of revolutionary warfare through their proxies, the Soviet Union is bring-

ing home painfully to us the limits of the *static* arms control
model to deter, compel, or contain a determined and aggressive
political adversary intent on changing the world balance of
power in its favor. (It is in the ability to force onto one's opponent
the decision to escalate conflict or concede that "strategic superiority" in the nuclear age matters.) If we fail to preserve an ambiguous counterforce capability to invoke the genuine deterrent
dangers of preemptive escalation, and continue to permit the
mutation of our conventional military forces into mere retaliatory forces, we will soon be forced into one-sided, formal
arms accommodations as the only "rational" response of a very
vulnerable people to continued Soviet military assertion, a response incipient in the Carter administration concessions on the
SS-18 missiles and the Backfire bombers. The deterring pressures
of accidental escalation, through two decades of policies to magnify our own vulnerabilities, will have come full circle to deter
us from taking the risks to preserve both our domestic unity and
our worldwide political interests.

## The Model and Our Allies

The crisis management model permits the threat of escalation
into even nuclear war to deter at grand levels and thus induce
bargaining, but only the incremental, retaliatory use of conventional armed force to induce bargaining among combatants at
"local" levels. There has been only one ally that we have ever
entertained protecting through deterrent threat of escalation into
nuclear conflict, and as General de Gaulle made clear to us in the
1960s, even this commitment to Western Europe has not appeared iron-clad. Indeed, it has been the increasing doubts about
our commitment to *deter* armed aggression in central Europe
through the credible commitment and capability to escalate conflict (exacerbated by recent calls for a "no first use" policy on
nuclear weapons by four eminent crisis managers[20]) that has
contributed to the successes of the European unilateralist movements.

The fortunes of the rest of our allies under the crisis management model have been relegated to the realm of incremental force
in punitive retaliation, controlled insofar as possible by crisis
management elites. Except where our allies have presented us
with a fait accompli as the Israelis did, for example, in the
preemptive strike on the Iraqi nuclear reactor, we have de-

manded that they react only punitively to faits accomplis inflicted upon them. (If Argentina had been outside the Western bloc, would we ever have permitted the British the latitude to handle their military operations in such a military fashion, e.g., isolating the battle area?)

The 1973 war between Israel and Egyptian-Syrian forces is an interesting case of the extension of the crisis management model beyond the Kennedy-Johnson administrations. In the hands of Secretary of State Kissinger our policies looked more than ever like the diplomacy of European monarchs resurrected and regarbed for the nuclear age, this time as catalysts for historical progress. Together with our partner in détente, the Soviet Union, we would manage this crisis in such a way as to swing the advantage in postwar mid-East diplomacy to ourselves, while permitting none of the belligerents to attain serious military victory (despite heavy losses), thus opening up new horizons for "creative" solutions in the area. This kind of logic *very nearly resulted*, according to Kissinger's own account, in the physical presence of both U.S. and Soviet forces in the battle area to "manage the crisis," and in *U.S. resupply(!)* of the trapped Egyptian third army when the Israelis resisted the logic of the crisis management model after incurring heavy losses from the surprise attack by Egypt and Syria. But perhaps most distressing here is the public avowal in his memoirs by a former U.S. Secretary of State of his admiration of Anwar Sadat for using massive military force and inflicting heavy casualties creatively for the limited aim of loosening up a dead-locked bargaining process![21]

The effects of these kinds of lessons in monarchic diplomacy upon the defensive alliances of this republic are clear enough. The system of defensive alliances we established throughout the world in the 1950s to contain Soviet military expansion are falling apart not simply because the Soviet Union now has a massive nuclear capability, but because, first, in the case of allies outside of NATO we have demonstrated that we intend to allow them to use force only punitively in retaliation, and after the fact, to stabilize conflict, not to defend themselves through elimination of the ability of the attacker to inflict casualties; second, within NATO, we are beginning to create the impression that we are no longer capable and resolved enough to *deter* Soviet aggression through threat of uncontrollable, preemptive escalation into nuclear war; and third, under the Nixon-Kissinger policies of détente with the Soviet Union, we institutionally seemed to have forgotten that while economic deprivations can start wars, commercial cooperation cannot deter them if there are more important issues at stake. When things become serious, only the ability to defend can ward off and defend. (In this sense, there must certainly not be another Vietnam in Central America.)

## Soviet Reaction to the Model

The attempt in the crisis management model to use the dangers of uncontrollable escalation into nuclear war as the basis for deterring all armed aggression has unfortunately worked to the favor of those revolutionary strategists, the leaders of the Soviet Union, by gradually leading the West to the disarming view that not only nuclear war, but all war is mad or insane and cannot be linked to policy. As Clausewitz carefully analyzed in *On War*, the activity of war itself does not begin with the attack, whose aim is simply possession or control, but in the interaction that arises when the attacked choose to *defend* themselves.[22] This means that *if* war at any level is insane (since it might lead to spasm nuclear war), then defense is also insane since it starts wars, carefully speaking, and even leads to escalation in the intensity of fighting (at least initially). This is, of course, what the crisis management model implies in its doctrine for the use of conventional armed force solely as a gradual and punitive retaliatory instrument, employed only after the fact to induce bargaining. To attempt to defend seriously or disarm the enemy might lead to genuine escalation of conflict.

Now, if the retaliatory use of force were capable of preserving its political foundations in the face of the decisive military use of force, it might be a possible policy for the security of ourselves and our allies in the nuclear age. But, as the Vietnam war made clear, the punitive use of firepower to preserve the opposing sovereign power and induce bargaining cannot, by itself, and for long, achieve political goals against an independent and determined enemy using military force to destroy the opposing political authority. Because the dangers of accidental war seem to deter at only grand levels, the choices at the level of aggressive guerrilla operations (or lower levels of conflict and terrorism) seem to be either genuine defense or withdrawal and accommodation.

And it is here that we can start to glimpse what those avid readers of Lenin and Clausewitz, the Soviet politburo, glimpsed (to judge by their policies of two decades) when they came to realize that the West was serious about the policy of security in the nuclear age through the dangers of mutual assured destruction (accidentally invoked). All they had to do was avoid unnecessary confrontation and bide their time; continue to build up their armed forces at all levels (to force the West to accommodate or escalate at each operational level); and proclaim policies of nuclear deterrence, arms control, and "socialist peace" (taking possession through terror is still not war), while covertly supporting revolutionary warfare worldwide. Over time the West would disarm itself through its own policy model. This could be expected to occur as it was gradually picked apart throughout the world by incremental revolution, terrorism, and insurgency, not subject to the deterrent dangers of escalation into nuclear war; became itself so vulnerable psychologically and physically that it could no longer credibly invoke the dangers of accidental war as a deterrent at higher levels of confrontation; and no longer possessed the conventional military force capabilities for decisive military action in major land warfare. And all this flowing from two decades of teaching the people in a popularly elected system of government that all war is mad in the nuclear age; hence defense is mad; hence military forces and weapons to defend political authority are mad. The ultimate result is frustration and diminishing effective opposition to a world revolutionary power that knows how to "strike the sovereign softly" (and simultaneously to nullify our ability to coerce through threat of conflict escalation by development of massive military capabilities at *all* operational levels). An additional implication is that if the Soviets *are* pursuing defense in the nuclear age, then they too are mad and, if anything, are to be excused their military actions on these grounds (i.e., "insanity defense," etc.).

## Conclusions

I have tried to show, by simply describing it, the existence and deleterious influence of a paradigm of thought I have called the crisis management model for security in the nuclear age. Formulated largely by American civilian intellectuals in and out of government, and evolving in the interaction with already existent domestic and foreign military realities, it came to be a ruling paradigm during the Kennedy administration, which has endured in part up to the current administration and has established the basic outline and horizon of our military, diplomatic, and foreign policies for two decades now.

I have tried to show, by indicating how it works, that this model contains a fundamental contradiction—to magnify our vulnerabilities while relying upon the deterrent threat of accidental or preemptive escalation—that over time and against an unaccommodating adversary is self-defeating politically and militarily. In two subsequent essays, I explore more deeply the long-range political errors in the model. In conclusion to this essay, I simply note that if our citizens and allies are to be consolidated behind a unified foreign policy, it will be necessary to arrest the magnification of our vulnerabilities in the face of accidental war, *while preserving its deterrent possibility,* and building and training the conventional armed forces *capable* of preserving political authority by defeating or at least controlling "local" military aggression throughout the world if required. In combination with genuine measures to limit future arms production (severed from the requirement to be the primary basis for national security), these measures might help our Soviet adversaries to see some advantage in preserving rather than altering the world balance of power.

1983

## Notes

1. "Special Message on the Defense Budget," submitted to Congress, 20 March 1961, *Public Papers of the Presidents of the U.S., J.F.K., Jan. 20–Dec. 21, 1961* (Washington, D. C.: U.S. Government Printing Office, 1962), 229–40.

2. Carefully speaking, the model requires creating the *illusion* of pressures toward uncontrollable escalation to intimidate the adversary, while taking concrete steps to eliminate that possibility. An example is the naval "quarantine" of Cuba during the 1962 "missile crisis."

3. As the United States has become more vulnerable, crisis management discussion of the dangers of accidental war has become more explicit. For examples of the genre, see Arthur Cox, *Russian Roulette* (New York: Times Books, 1982), esp. chap. 1, "Accidental Nuclear War;" and Louis Beres, *Apocalypse* (Chicago: University of Chicago Press, 1980).

4. See Bernard Brodie's 1946 essay, "The Weapon," in *The Absolute Weapon* (Freeport, N.Y.: Books for Libraries Press, 1972), esp. 28 and 75.

5. See, in this connection, Albert Wohlstetter, "The Delicate Balance of Terror," *Foreign Affairs* 37, no. 2 (January 1959): 211–34.

6. This is one of the assumptions of economic game theory as applied to potential nuclear conflict. See, for example, Thomas Schelling, *The Strategy of Conflict* (Cambridge: Harvard University Press, 1960), and Lawrence Freedman, *The Evolution of Nuclear Strategy* (New York: St. Martin's Press, 1981), esp. chap. 12.

7. My formulation of this paradigm is a synthesis of explicit arguments, implications of those arguments, and observations of our actual conduct under crisis management direction. Two books that (if read discerningly) will be found to contain much of the essence of the paradigm, are Schelling, *Arms and Influence*, and Robert McNamara, *The Essence of Security* (New York: Harper and Row, 1968). On the meaning of "limited war," see the subsequently influential essays in Walter Kaufmann, ed., *Military Policy and National Security* (Princeton: Princeton University Press, 1956). Still perhaps more telling in this connection is Robert McNamara's remark in November 1962, that "There is no longer any such thing as strategy, only crisis management," cited in *The Harper Dictionary of Modern Thought* (New York: Harper and Row, 1978), 144–45.

8. These military principles are traditional and commonsensical, and could be found in a book such as Clausewitz's *On War*, or the military field manuals of the U.S. Army until the 1976 operations manual. (The 1982 basic operations manual is a great improvement in this regard, but still makes the logical error of asserting that the primary mission of our armed forces is to deter war, rather than aid in a political policy of deterrence through the capability to defeat, disarm, or control enemy forces if deterrence were to fail or threaten to fail. See the first sentence of Department of the Army publication *FM 100-5/Operations*, 1982, i.)

9. This outline of events in the Cuban missile crisis is taken primarily from the narrative construction by Alexander George in "The Cuban Missile Crisis, 1962," in George, et al., *The Limits of Coercive Diplomacy* (Boston: Little, Brown and Co., 1971), 86–143.

10. For a similar understanding of the crisis, see Peter Rodman, "The Missiles of October: Twenty Years Later," in *Commentary* (October 1982): 39–45.

11. For a lengthy investigation of "coercive bargaining" and the North Vietnamese (non)reaction to it, see Wallace J. Thies, *When Governments Collide: Coercion and Diplomacy in the Vietnam Conflict, 1964–68* (Berkeley: University of California Press, 1980), esp. 222–83.

12. For a "day-by-day" account of the "air war" until 1968, see Thies, *When Governments Collide*.

13. For a discussion of "fire-base psychosis," see Dave Palmer, *Summons of the Trumpet: U.S.-Vietnam in Perspective* (Novato, Cal.: Presidio Press, 1978), esp. 143: "Infantry units were all but forbidden to practice their traditional mission of closing with . . . the enemy . . . maneuver elements *found* the foe while firepower eliminated him."

14. For a military comparison of the Korean and Vietnam cases, see Harry Summers, *On Strategy: A Critical Analysis of the Vietnam War* (Novato, Cal.: Presidio Press, 1982), 165–69.

15. For a discussion of the organizational changes effected by and after Secretary McNamara, see Victor Krulak, *Organizing for National Security* (Washington D.C.: U.S. Strategic Institute, 1983).

16. This kind of language occurred even in official memoranda. See, for example, "Memorandum for the President by McNamara, April 21, 1965," in *Vietnam: A History in Documents*, ed. G. Porter (New York: New American Library, 1979), 309–10.

17. See Palmer, *Summons of the Trumpet*, and Edward Luttwak, "Western Europe Needs a Nuclear Option," in *The Apocalyptic Premise*, ed. E. Lefever and E. Hunt (Washington, D.C.: Ethics and Public Policy Center, 1982), 47–61.

18. For insight into the original aims of "arms control," see Donald Brennan,

ed., *Arms Control, Disarmament, and National Security* (New York: George Braziller, 1961), esp. the essay by Thomas Schelling, "Reciprocal Measures for Arms Stabilization," 167–86; and Thomas Schelling and Morton Halperin, *Strategy and Arms Control* (New York: The Twentieth Century Fund, 1961). For an especially candid expression of the hopes for arms control, see the foreword by Paul Warnke to Beres's book *Apocalypse*, which contains the following assertion: "Nuclear war is incompatible with human existence, *and only arms control can prevent it from happening.*" (p. xiii, emphasis added.)

19. The arguments of Immanuel Kant's famous little essay on perpetual peace are strikingly similar in outline to the arguments recurring in the principal crisis management journal, *International Security;* both reflect a historical view that while war may once have been a catalyst for human progress, this is no longer the case owing to the destructiveness of modern weapons, and thus the need for accelerated enlightment and evolution of the species.

20. See McGeorge Bundy, George Kennan, Robert McNamara, and Gerard Smith, "Nuclear Weapons and the Atlantic Alliance," *Foreign Affairs* (Spring 1982): 753–68.

21. See Henry Kissinger's account of the 1973 war in the second volume of his memoirs, *Years of Upheaval* (Boston: Little, Brown and Co., 1982), chap. 12–13, 545–666.

22. Carl von Clausewitz, *On War*, ed. and trans. Michael Howard and Peter Paret (Princeton: Princeton University Press, 1976), bk. 6, 1–12, 357–408.

# 7

# Armed Force and Republican Government

The previous essay directed attention to the misguided attempt in the crisis management model to base our national security and the protection of our vital interests in the nuclear age upon the threat of magnified vulnerability to the dangers of accidental escalation. (Again, have any but the naive ever believed in the deterrent effect of the public doctrine of punitive retaliation after the fact?) And it has not been difficult to find public support for our natural commercial military disinclinations. There have been few public outcries over the absence of civil defense measures; over the attempt to establish professional, voluntary military forces; or about the vague impression given by crisis management elites that their control of advanced weapons technology could guarantee security with little sacrifice. Nevertheless, the absence of much public resistance in this matter (at least until the present administration) does not absolve our leadership of failing to perform its proper political function of reminding a commercial people of their military disinclinations rather than encouraging these as they began to grow into imbalance—and as the basis for national security! This essay will try to show the dangers in the crisis management model for our system of government, by shedding some light on a dark corner of our memory—the once well-understood role of armed force in the republican balance.

Can the word "republic" have any practical meaning for us in an age in which it is claimed by countries as diverse as the United States and China? It does already if we think about it; why else do we feel discomfort at the use of "republic" and "democratic republic" to describe authoritarian communist systems like the Chinese and East German? Although the exact meaning of "republic" has always been disputed—mixed government, balanced government, popular government, representative democracy, public virtue, primacy of domestic policy?—there is still an abiding if elusive content to the idea of a republic that, for us as Americans, is worth analyzing from time to time. I would suggest that the most universal yet undiluted definition of the term, and one that goes to the heart of the common part of its meaning, is that of balanced government, or simply balance. Regardless of the *exact* form of government intended by the term throughout the ages, it has been intended to produce (and in turn be perpetuated by) the ideal of balance. In our case, this took the form of the citizen who minds both his own profession *and* the public things, rather than a balancing of classes.

This suggests a limit to the idea of balance. It suggests that most citizens can do one thing well—their own craft or profession—and still have sufficient energy to stay familiar with public issues, make necessary sacrifices, and choose intelligently their political representatives and leaders. As a practical idea, "republic" then begins to distinguish itself from any sort of class or specialized system in which one group reserves to itself the right and skill to rule (monarchy, aristocracy, tyranny, oligarchy); or from a system in which everybody claims the right and skill to do everything else (e.g., Marx's early vision of communist democracy); or from one in which *everybody* does just one thing and ruling becomes the contingent outcome of their various competitions (e.g., "free market capitalism"); or from one in which *every group* does just one thing and ruling becomes the contingent outcome of their various competitions (e.g., "interest group democracy").

The danger in the crisis management model of national and world security for this kind of republican government is that it calculatedly begins to distance the majority of middle-class citizens (some of whom will at one time help rule in one of the three branches of government, national or local) from familiarity with one of the unavoidable public things, the use of armed (and unarmed) force in defense. By attempting to guarantee security through technological contrivances (i.e., magnified vulnerability in the face of the dangers of accidental, preemptive escalation), in conjunction with limited covert and counterinsurgent operations in local hot spots, it risks losing the conventional main-force skills and organization, as well as the habit and willingness of the majority of middle-class citizens, to support military efforts. ("Why make great sacrifices for small stakes?") In addition to the military risk here, there is also involved a political risk, attendant to specialization by one group in the use of armed force. This is

the danger that we will begin to mutate into an empire, or at least
an imperial republic, as we have already been called by some.

This change might not show at first in the forms of our government, but it would show in the composition and aims of our
military forces, in the kind of foreign policy we conduct, and in
the personalities of both our leaders and the voters who elect
them. This last development is the most worrisome from a political standpoint since republican government seems to require a
moderate relationship to armed force. Anytime that most citizens
are led to either great unfamiliarity with armed force, or to great
preoccupation with it, there occurs a change in both the external
and internal organization of the life of a body politic, which
amounts to a change in its constitution. As general possibilities,
in the former case there is the danger of dictatorship and loss of
freedom through either internal takeover by an unopposed
praetorian guard, or external takeover by a conquering army or its
threat. In the latter case, if a people becomes thoroughly preoc-
cupied with military ways, either from necessity or inclination,
political association gradually mutates into military association
as the freedom of citizens under general laws is squeezed into
the more confining proportions of soldiers' duties under military
directive. We recognize this trend during extraordinary national
emergencies when civil life is temporarily suspended in the
invocation of marital or emergency law. And, in addition to the
more obvious twentieth-century totalitarian examples of this development in the extreme, one might also cite the case of the
Roman republic, which it has been suggested began mutation
into the empire as it increased the military organization of its
civil life to compete militarily with the Carthaginians.[1]

The ideal of balanced citizenry then has been the mainstay of
republican stability, whether in older, mixed regimes where the
middle class acted as a buffer between rich and poor, or in our
own extended, commercial republic where the middle class has
been the largest and most important political element on its own
merits. This balance has been maintained both in the external
organization of our public life and, in turn, in the internal ordering of the personalities of citizens, and each has nurtured the life
of the other. In addition to other and higher things, an indispensable part of this balance has been until recently the heretofore
abiding insight that there were unavoidable moments or times
("to everything a season") when it was necessary to resort to force
in order to preserve integrity—that is, a consistent way of meet-

ing change that gave identity and meaning to one's life, or the life of a people. The fortitude (and know-how) to defend oneself and one's own in both word and deed, if necessary, was a part of our civic ideal of individual and national independence, and was nurtured in families as one attribute of masculine character; was a moral lesson taught in schools in compilations like the McGuffey readers, and in organized sports; recurred in films; was upheld in courts in doctrines of self-defense; and was the legitimation for military service, and for the doctrine and organization of our military forces. Externally it demanded the training to be skillful and effective in the use of force; internally it demanded the fortitude to function, and continue to function, under conditions of physical danger and deprivation. Together, and in combination with other attributes, these contributed to a civic ideal of spirited independence.

The crisis management model of national and world security through policies of magnified vulnerability, and employment of elite and covert forces like the "green berets" and the CIA, threaten, in combination with the natural disposition of this commercial republic, to eliminate this aspect of our republican balance. By eliminating the military basis to attempt the common defense in the nuclear age, and through what amount to academic and media conspiracies of silence on the historical role of defense in the preservation of political liberty, the crisis management model works to undermine the basis for political leadership to balance our more private and selfish (and economically productive!) tendencies by invocation of the abiding requirements of national defense. This is worrisome not only militarily and psychologically, but in a broad political sense as well, because it seems to have been the unavoidable requirements of military defense that have managed to transform mere capitalist economies into liberal polities, by bringing into power and influence from time to time leaders (Lincoln and Churchill, for example) who recognize the minimal requirements for a structure of political authority grounded in some principle other than simply facilitation of fruitful commerce and private transaction. Such leaders, by influencing both moral ideals and government organization and hiring practices, manage to tilt the commercial tendency back into balance with the requirements of public spiritedness. This is done by politically and rhetorically skillful direction of public attention toward a genuine external danger. Yet the crisis management model and those political leaders and opinion makers under its sway continue to try to magnify our people's physical and psychological vulnerabilities in the face of the genuine danger of Soviet military assertion and the real possibilities of unintended war.

What indications are there that the republican balance in some of our leaders and citizens, and with it the reasoned conviction that there are things in life worth preserving through some risk to life itself, is being lost in the use of a policy model designed to avoid nuclear war at all costs? This is an elusive question and one difficult to find demonstration for. One could attempt citing evidence like the increasing numbers of junior legislators and judges without previous military service; one could cite the novel view of many citizens and judges that capital punishment for capital crimes is now "cruel and unusual"; or the increasingly narrow conditions under which our courts will justify the use of armed and even unarmed force in even personal defense; or the decreasing frequency with which the moral lessons of classical, Jewish, and early Christian authors (e.g., St. Augustine) justifying the use of armed force in the common defence are taught in the public schools, or the ease with which the appellation "fascist" is falsely and casually applied in public discussion to any forceful invocation of governmental authority; or the growing assumption that anger is always a psychological aberration. But alternative explanations could probably be cited for any one of these developments, even if they were admitted to be occurring. And they are more accurately seen as symptoms rather than causes of our political imbalance, although they contribute to it as they grow unchecked.

The appropriate demonstration of a political development is at the level of policy. The fundamental problem here is a growing inability and disinterest on the part of the majority of American middle-class citizens to make competent, commonsensical judgements about the use of armed force in national policy, because they have had their common sense subverted over two decades through application of a crisis management policy model which tells them that security rests upon increased vulnerability; tailors our defense and military forces to achieve that end; used conventional armed force ineptly and expensively in Vietnam; and supports, for its own reasons, the aims of pacifists, clergymen, and educators, that is, abiding human characters who have always believed that spiritedness, anger, and the use of force to defend one's own were fundamentally inhuman attributes making for spirited defense. Still, if the principles of political liberty upon which our government was founded are to endure through the nuclear age, it must remain the task of our political leadership to make morally meaningful, and militarily feasible, the defense of our way of life. For, it is unlikely, given the long history of independence and individualism as civic ideals in this country, that it will be politically or psychologically possible for the middle class to opt out of its own defense through exclusive reliance on crisis management—that is, arms control techniques and small, professional, paramilitary forces. The continued attempt to do so threatens to divide the country to the point of dangerous paralysis in its external defense. Nor does it seem likely that we can mutate successfully into some sort of "imperial" republic in which white-collar workers employ the blue-collar workers and social misfits to do their fighting for them. Either there will be the social divisiveness associated with the Vietnam war, since the attempt goes against our ideals of political equality and fair play; or, in an attempt to avoid this development and maintain the appearance of equality of duties, the refusal to become involved militarily at some critical point somewhere when we must.

Yet there is an even more fundamental reason why the (especially upper) middle class must be weaned from the illusion that it can rule and lead without understanding of, and training in, the use of armed force. To lead successfully, it must have knowledge of the *full* range of human things, including the use of armed force and the way people behave in the presence of it. If one searches for a broad explanation of the mistakes of the Vietnam war, they are to be found in the insufficient knowledge of human nature in war (whether owing to visionary hopes, lack of experience, or both) of the Kennedy intellectuals who made the crisis management model into a ruling paradigm. (Recall Sam Rayburn's remark in 1960 that he would feel better if just one of them had once been county sheriff.)

The reasons for this illusion are not far to seek if we are permitted to deal in the political realm of common sense. Common sense is obviously not some sense common to all—if it were, the crisis management model could never have become ascendant. Nor is it some unlearned sense, although it may not be teachable to everyone. By common sense, we mean, if we think about it, the ability to bring together ("in common") in an instant the insights, information, and intuitions of all our senses and cognitions in order to make a judgment about the continued adaptation of the whole individual, or system, or organism. This is evident in our meaning when we describe as lacking common

sense someone who gives either insufficient attention to a significant matter, or too much attention to an insignificant matter, at
the expense of the continued functioning of the whole (like a
ship's captain busy with log entries when there is still a chance
to save his sinking ship). It is obviously *the* political sense, since
politics in the broad sense is the "common" activity of ordering
priorities among all the other activities (legal, moral, military,
economic, spiritual) to permit the continued functioning of the
body politic. And it is evident in the tenacious persistence in our
use of the expression "common sense," despite the efforts of
scientists and logicians to lay it to rest, that it is describing a real
human faculty and we need it (both the thing and the expression
to describe it) to make sense of our experience.

If we are permitted, then, to deal in the realm of political
common sense, the reasons for the illusions of the formulators of
the crisis management are not far to seek. Motivated by genuine
concern to inject flexibility into what they considered a dan-
gerously rigid and "escalatory" integrated operations plan for
confrontational contingencies with the Soviet Union,[2] they quite
simply lost their balance and went overboard in an obsession for
absolute certainty and control over military mobilization procedures in developing crises. Rather than rely upon political
leadership to control escalation of conflict in a confrontation
through assertion of authority, they attempted to devise a new set
of procedures that, as the previous essay discussed in detail,
would use the apparent dangers of escalation to contain the
dangers of escalation, *at all operational levels*. Crisis management elites, presumably in control of their own procedures and
to a great degree of nuclear weapons production specifications,
would preserve the security of the country by largely excluding
their own unpredictable populations from the new esoteric subject of crisis management; by controlling their own military
forces by inducing their mutation into limited security forces;
and by setting up such air-tight models of security through
proper nuclear weapons configuration ("arms control") that Soviet leaders could presumably have little coercive effect on our
procedures unless they were willing to initiate mutual suicide.
But, unfortunately, owing to their insufficient grasp of the relationship of authority and force, the apolitical Kennedy advisors
in (and out of) the McNamara "defense" department relied upon
a technological model of control to perform political and military
tasks that it is not in the nature of things to permit. Their errors,
which can be discerned in their incomplete psychology, can also

112 ARMED FORCE AND REPUBLICAN GOVERNMENT

be traced in the visible, political and military effects of two decades of the rule of their paradigm. In the previous essay, I traced the politico-military errors of the model; here I will try to trace its politico-psychological ones.

The fundamental political problem in the crisis management model of national security is that in the interest of detailed certainty and control over all levels of diplomacy and armed operations to contain escalation, it attempts seriously to curtail the authority, initiative, and responsibility of high and intermediate level military commanders (and diplomatic representatives), while downplaying the importance of all political authority, including that of the president of the United States when it is seen to conflict with technological imperatives deemed necessary to avoid nuclear war. (As the sixth essay indicated, the deterrent *uncertainty* in the dangers of preemptive escalation by ambiguous counterforce weapons systems would be managed exclusively by high-level crisis managers.) Our conduct of the Vietnam war is illustrative of the first trend; the role in its downfall of the increasing foreign policy isolation of the Nixon-Kissinger White House is illustrative of the latter.

In brief, the dramatic appeal of a model for technological management (with high presumed certainty) of the dangers of both intentional and unintentional nuclear war has given wide-scale support it might never have otherwise received to a political and pyschological tendency already afoot in the aims of both modern science and the mass politics of "resentment." That tendency is the attempt, for various reasons, to externalize, make "visible," and control insofar as possible, *all* the forces of the human psyche. In the case of modern science this is necessary for the standardization, reproduction, and progressive accumulation of objective measures (ultimately quantitative) of man and the physical universe; in the case of the politics of "resentment," standardized measures of worth are necessary to restrain the political, social, and economic rewards accruing to the immeasurable and inequal talents of creativity, genius, courage, and so forth; and in the case of the crisis management model, an externalized, incremental, measurable basis for policy is deemed necessary for the control of escalation procedures in developing crises. Together these trends all conspire critically to undermine the perceived need for political (and military) authority, the only basis there has ever been for *moderate* control and productive channeling of the irrational forces of the human psyche—passion, creativity, and anger. The alternative experimental and utopian solutions are all insufficiently tolerant of that healthy liberty necessary for their nourishment.

It is clearly outside the subject of this essay to pursue further the implications for creativity and passion of the attempt to externalize the *psyche*. (See, in this connection, the ninth essay of this book.) Yet, the demonstrable and refutable errors of the crisis management model's attempt to deny by implication in its policy assumptions the existence and force of "spirited" anger and courage in the human psyche, and the need for its traditional mechanisms of control—that is, political authority grounded in the capability for skillful use of armed force—go some way in pointing out the practical limits of this unhealthy, psychic project. (It is culminating already in public articulations like the operant psychologist B. F. Skinner's *Beyond Freedom and Dignity*, and its explicit call to eliminate the "inner autonomous man" and his resistance to environmental manipulation, in the name of world survival.)

The crisis management model is based ultimately upon an incomplete and economic, or appetitive, psychology of man; and, in turn, upon unrealistic assumptions about its ability to separate enemy leadership from enemy forces and population. There is no other way to explain its errors short of a calculated attempt to deceive our own people in the interest of avoiding nuclear war at all costs. (The pragmatic problem is that if it results in sufficient political instability in America and its allies, it may actually increase the dangers of unintended war by provoking us into a crisis we are no longer militarily strong enough to control abroad, nor politically strong enough to control at home as perceptions and pressures of vulnerability mount.) The model's incomplete psychology is apparent in its rationale for the incremental use of force to inflict pain gradually upon an enemy until his leadership calculates rationally that the threat and risk of escalated (and possibly uncontrollable) conflict is a worse alternative than negotiating differences at the bargaining table. This was the rationale of the McNamara advisors for our incremental bombing campaign in North Vietnam to browbeat the enemy into negotiations.[3]

The most extended attempt at a justification for our incremental "strategy" (distinguished from a decisive strategy for limited aims) in Vietnam is to be found in former McNamara advisor T. C. Schelling's *Arms and Influence*, a very influential book, continuously in print since 1966. As an economist, Schelling begins with the bold assertion that the entire history of warfare has really been about a kind of coercive bargaining—the infliction of pain for desired political and economic outcomes.[4] When punitive infliction is *calculated* to have become sufficiently undesirable, concessions are made. Ignoring political and moral ends (Schelling's economic vocabulary cannot distinguish the activity of the U.S. Army from that of the mafia), and ignoring the history of skillful strategic and tactical use of armed force to *make* enemy forces do something (i.e., physically *control* them), Schelling treats all warfare as a variation of what has been called attrition warfare. Yet, he misconstrues the nature of even attrition warfare by arguing that there is some calculated break-even point when the cost of pain becomes too great. This is not what occurs in even attrition warfare (except possibly among pre-Napoleonic monarchs fighting colonial wars with mercenary armies), not even as a piece of somewhat removed analysis.

What does occur in attrition warfare between nations is that the physical and moral effects of armed force (i.e., destruction and *shock*) are used *to induce a state of pliability* in enemy forces and leadership in order to obtain a desired political outcome, prior to actual physical control over them (e.g., the conclusion of the war with Japan through population bombing). This view that increments of pain are added up in some utilitarian calculus is simply nonsense. As anyone with experience in even the unarmed use of force knows, once violence is used, opponents are either reduced to an incapacitating state of moral and/or medical shock, or they become even more spirited, angry, and determined. Nor is the situation essentially different for states and armies; it is rather that dimensions expand to include debilitating shock—that is, absence of a pattern where one was expected—in the system of political and military authority as well.

The economic model of trading increments of pain makes sense only so long as pain is talked about (thus, it is somewhat more applicable to discussions of nuclear deterrence); once pain is actually felt, there is either incapacitation, or a leap to a more spirited level of resolve and purpose, as was apparent in the reactions of the North Vietnamese to our highly self-limited bombing campaign. The only time bombing in North Vietnam was ever done in a sustained and military fashion to induce widespread shock was during the eleven days of "Linebacker II" as part of President Nixon's attempt to get the North Vietnamese back to the negotiating table in December 1972, in order that we might continue to withdraw our troops. Observers in both Hanoi and Paris report that the effect was quite demoralizing and debilitating, and temporarily broke the enemy's will to fight.[5]

Either, then, Mr. McNamara and his advisors like Professor Schelling did not understand the effect of physical, moral, and political shock in obtaining desired political concessions through use of armed force even in attrition war (which seems rather unlikely); or they mistakenly calculated that they could separate enemy leadership from enemy forces and population by incremental pain infliction on the latter but not the former in Hanoi; or they mistakenly calculated that they could at least stabilize the entire situation by establishing a U.S. "military" presence without a military purpose to reduce and justify its sacrifices against an aggressive enemy. Above all else, they could not afford to induce shock in the North Vietnamese political leadership according to the crisis management paradigm they followed, because shock is irrational, and might actually lead to an uncontrollable situation. Now, this is a possible way of conducting foreign policy and warfare in the abstract, not dissimilar in effect from the policies of European monarchs prior to the Napoleonic revolution. But as the American domestic reaction to its losses in Vietnam made clear, it is not viable foreign policy for a republican government whose citizens are neither accustomed to making, nor prepared to make, the sacrifices of war without serious political aims to justify them, and serious military measures to minimize them.

What is the connection between the incomplete psychology of the crisis management model and its aversion to assertion of authority, initiative, and latitude of action by both our military forces, and by the supposedly sovereign states we are assisting? The fear that independence at lower operational levels may lead to real, uncontrollable escalation is obvious enough, but there is more involved here than that. The requirement in the model for certainty and control over the technology and procedures that could lead to enlarged conflict have led it to embrace an incomplete vocabulary and psychology of man under conditions of war, which denies reality by accounting for only a part of it. The real opponent of the crisis management model, regardless of the extent to which its formulators have seen it, is the irrational, spirited part of the human *psyche* that comes into play especially in war; that cannot be measured in increments; and that can be controlled sustainedly only by an institutionalized refinement of itself—the assertion of political authority and resolve, grounded in the (credible) capabilities of our armed forces to control (not persuade) hostile forces. Not only does the crisis management model have no vocabulary or concepts for this part of human experience, but it does not even attempt to legitimate the control of crisis management elites in these terms. Their claim to manage crises is predicated on their ability to achieve desired outcomes, most supremely the avoidance of war, while protecting U.S. national interests in the area of conflict. This proclaimed ability to manage crises, in turn, is grounded on mastery of the presumed techniques of coercive bargaining and previously applied arms control—that is, control over the composition of nuclear forces, and other forces. (Ironically, crisis managers have often talked of the need for "resolve" during crises; but what this means is the resolve of crisis managers to allow neither their own population nor enemy forces to become politically resolved to defend, by "holding the line" until the perception of their own vulnerabilities dawns on both belligerent parties, *or at least the more vulnerable of them,* and leads to accommodations.)

The problem here with the crisis management model, evident in the decline over the past two decades of our government's credibility, and our relative bargaining position throughout the world, is that by beginning with a self-induced partiality or blindness about the human *psyche,* it forgoes the likelihood of being successful in areas of its blindness. By starting with psychological assumptions appropriate perhaps to commercial and technological activities but not to high-level politics, diplomacy, and war, it diminishes its ability to be successful in these latter activities that involve a fuller range of human experience. Instead of seeing the indispensability of political authority in civilized life, and using our technological advances to enhance it, the model in effect tries to substitute technological for political control, in the supreme interest of certainty and control over a putative escalation process, and to the detriment of our credibility and influence throughout the world. The technological advance of the helicopter as a speedy and maneuverable gunship and troop transport in Vietnam, for example, made it almost impossible for the North Vietnamese to mount against us successfully the kind of siege and ambush operations that defeated the French at Dien Ben Phu in 1954. Yet the individual successes of air cavalry and air mobile units could not by themselves achieve our political aims in Vietnam because under the crisis management model we refused to use armed force to establish and consolidate a system of authority on the ground, or permit a sovereign South Vietnamese government to do so. (And eventually our own Congress cut off crucial promised aid out of understandable, but unjustifiable, frustration.)[6]

At a more general level, the model and its economic psychology squander the diversity of talent in this country, and confuse the tasks of political leadership by helping bring into political power, and intrenching in the bureaucracy, *in all seasons*, individuals both whose instincts and policy models encourage the apolitical commercial and technological tendencies of this country rather than healthily resist them when they venture into inappropriate areas. (This description does not well fit the current administration on the question of defense, but they have hardly vanquished the crisis management paradigm, perhaps not even fully yet discerned it.) As Tocqueville made clear for us in *Democracy in America*, the preservation of our political balance, as a people with strong commercial and private tendencies, requires that we maintain a tension between those democratic desires and the obligations of public-spirited sacrifice. The crisis management model as a ruling paradigm, by challenging the legitimacy of providing for the common defense and basing security, in part, on the deterrent effects of magnified fear and vulnerability of our people, works to slacken this spirited tension between private comfort and public sacrifice, which transforms a people in mere physical proximity into a body politic. Acceptance of the crisis management assumptions is not so much won from more commonsensical citizens, but their resistance to these assumptions is diminished as they see fewer, viable institutional alternatives for channeling their own energies. If any administration is to loosen the crisis management model from its hold over American foreign and defense policy, the assumptions of the model must be made publicly explicit in order that informed debate can ensue. Such debate, in turn, could help reright the republican balance of the country by bringing back into the common defense the intellectual and emotional energies of the majority of citizens.

I have not meant to suggest the United States rid itself of the CIA, the "green berets," or all crisis management and arms control techniques. There are seasons when these are appropriate. Rather, I have meant to suggest that these be deprived of their centrality in the provision of our national security, in the return to policies in which we would ground deterrence upon the perceived ability to attempt our defense if deterrence were to fail at conventional and guerrilla force levels, or threaten to fail at nuclear force levels. Regardless of the exact forms and policies to achieve this general aim, the attempt would mean the inclusion of the majority of citizens in defense debate and participation as the best bet for the political stability to give nuclear deterrence and political freedom a life over generations.

Such a general policy aim might also help to clarify for us what our foreign policy aims as a republic ought to be. Ever since Woodrow Wilson started calling us a democracy in World War I, and got us interested in making the world safe for it, there has been confusion at the level of our world image about what we stand for. When we talked of ourselves as a federal republic, or even a federal democratic republic, our meaning was fairly clear—we were a territorially extended and legally decentralized system of representative government preserved through institutional checks and balances. This system of government was seen as the best hope for a self-perpetuating arrangement to allow the greatest number of individuals to realize their natural potential over time. And if we were a species of democracy or popular government, it was a form of *political* democracy that prudentially filtered the popular will through hierarchic and rather complex arrangements of authority, distinguished from "populist" democracy to enact the popular will at any moment, or "economic democracy" to guarantee a job to every citizen through pervasive governmental regulation.

Yet in embracing the unqualified term "democracy" (or sometimes the expression "liberal" democracy" whose constitutional meaning is unclear), we confused ourselves and the world about our aims, and forced ourselves into appearing to promise something different from what our constitutional and institutional arrangements could provide. In addition, as our world credibility has waned in the gap between our own system of government and the revolutionary expectations generated by the unqualified expression "democracy," we have responded usually by expressions of surprised hurt followed by even more unrealistic promises of what we can deliver especially to the countries of the "developing world."

The crisis management model with its requirements for strict operational control over all levels of diplomatic and military levels of activity (now mimicked by the legislative branch as well) has pushed us further in the direction of a standardizing democratic centralism, evidenced in our aversion to tolerating the genuine sovereignty of any nation we seriously begin to aid militarily (e.g., South Vietnam, Iran, El Salvador). This tendency is fueled as well by domestic pressures on policy makers and legislators from a United States population increasingly encouraged to think of democracy not as constitutional arrangements (i.e., a structure of authority legitimated by established procedures and a set of beliefs about their propriety), but as substantive outcomes like "economic and human rights" to be immediately provided and guaranteed.

To return to a public discussion and understanding of what our federal and republican system of government provides, distinguished from the standard of life that our citizens have over two centuries been able to secure for themselves under it, might not only clarify certain domestic issues, but give us guidelines for foreign and domestic policy that coincide with our political potential. It may turn out in such a public discussion that ours is a rarer form of government than we have imagined, made possible in part through natural gifts and advantages, and that it cannot simply be exported wholesale to largely agrarian countries throughout the world. And it may turn out that we can conduct a far more effective and credible foreign policy in the service of political and commercial freedom, by putting our own house in order and taking measures to relegitimate the general aim of providing for the common defense of ourselves and our sovereign allies, rather than attempting to enmesh them in a web of crisis management techniques. As we began to do this, U.S. policy makers might also find increased their abilities to deal with both unilateralism and terrorism worldwide.

To begin publicly to explain the duties of American citizens in their common defense, and to take measures to make them performable, would be admission that we were still a political people interested in the preservation of a set of constitutional arrangements under which the maximum liberty of citizens was made possible because they also minded, and sacrificed for, the public things. It would begin to correct a grand confusion of over two decades in which we have tried to ground our national security in the magnification of our own, and our allies', physical and psychological vulnerabilities. And it might remind both us and the world that there is still a living, republican alternative available between the mass, democratic tyrannies of both the benign and extreme varieties, grounded in beliefs about the legitimacy of authority, rather than in guarantees of certain substantial conditions, for example, avoidance of nuclear war *at all costs*.

1983

# Notes

1. Hans Delbrück, the German political-military historian, argued that the Roman republic began to mutate into the empire after the Second Punic War, when in order to defeat Hannibal, the Romans were forced into a professional rather than a citizen army: "The new military system, as created by Scipio . . . stood in basic contradiction to the Republic, and from now on Roman military history, and with it Roman history in general, moved within the framework of this innate contradiction." *History of the Art of War Within the Framework of Political History,* trans. Walter Renfroe, Jr. (Westport, Conn.: Greenwood Press, 1975; original German publication, 1900), vol. 1 ("Antiquity"), 412.

2. For an account of the reactions of the Kennedy advisors to "SIOP-62," see the story, "Why We Decided Not to Nuke the Soviets," *The Washington Post,* 29 May 1983, p. C–3.

3. For a lengthy account of the McNamara bombing policies, see Wallace J. Thies, *When Governments Collide: Coercion and Diplomacy in the Vietnam Conflict, 1964–68* (Berkeley: University of California Press, 1980).

4. Thomas Schelling, *Arms and Influence* (New Haven: Yale University Press, 1966), 1–34.

5. On the shock effects of the eleven days of sustained bombing of serious targets in North Vietnam, see Dave Palmer, *Summons of the Trumpet* (Novato, Cal.: Presidio Press, 1978), 259; and the letter to the editor of *The American Spectator* of June 1983 by Adm. James Bond Stockdale, a prisoner in Hanoi during the bombing. For an admission that, in order to induce final negotiations as part of our withdrawal, we were willing to induce shock in the enemy leadership, see Henry Kissinger, *White House Years* (Boston: Little, Brown and Co., 1979), 1446–57.

6. According to former President Nixon, after 1973 the United States cut promised aid to South Vietnam by over 75%, while the Soviet Union doubled its aid to North Vietnam. Richard Nixon, "Don't let Salvador Become Another Vietnam," editorial in *The Wall Street Journal,* 17 May 1983, p. 22.

# 8
# Armed Force and Political Liberty

We live in a time when normally healthy pacifist sentiment is rising to a dangerous level of political influence, as it receives less resistance from more commonsensical and balanced citizens in the United States and Western Europe. This development has occurred not merely from growing awareness of the vast potential destructiveness of nuclear weapons but, as I have tried to demonstrate, from the political and "military" policies of the crisis management model to magnify our physical and psychological vulnerabilities as the basis for a "deterrent" security. "If we are sufficiently vulnerable, how can we afford to engage in military confrontation or even its serious threat?" the model "reasons." Yet, as I have also tried to show, this model is self-defeating on pragmatic grounds alone, since the other half of its deterrent basis has been the credibility of uncontrollable, preemptive strikes (i.e., accidental war), and eventually this threat works to deter us rather than our opponents as we become the more vulnerable through crisis management policies of self-induced vulnerability. In time, with increasing one-sided vulnerability, our only solution to stability with an aggressive Soviet Union becomes unilateral disarmament and accommodation camouflaged to ourselves (not the world) in formal weapons negotiations. (This development reached alarming lengths during the Carter administration and, no doubt, contributed to its electoral defeat.)

The contradiction in the model has always been vaguely sensed by those who naively believe that deterrence has really been based upon the threat of punitive retaliation after the fact. If this were so, they reason correctly, why do we need even an ambiguous counterforce capability, why not rely upon "minimum deterrence"? Yet they have little answer to critics who point out the immorality of punitive retaliation that would become largely an act of revenge, or to more discerning critics who question whether we would ever use nuclear weapons solely for posthumous revenge.

In such a time, it is more important than ever that we understand clearly the role of defense and armed force in the achievement of our way of life. If we are going to abandon the attempt to defend ourselves, we ought to see clearly the major political and military ramifications of the choice before we make it (perhaps irrevocably). It may even occur that when we do, we may decide not to abandon the project of the common defense. In the previous essay I sketched some of the links between the use of armed force and the maintenance of republican political and psychological balance. In this essay I try to go some way in explaining the differences between the punitive use of armed force after the fact in retaliation (largely a civil police function), and the military use of armed force to defend before a fait accompli can be achieved. As I shall try to show, it is the latitude of freedom, initiative, and authority achieved in the latter (military) use of armed force that makes political liberty possible, and the use of armed force morally justifiable to large numbers of people. Subsequent to this theoretical distinction, I will explore briefly some of the problems created for the capability and use of defensive armed force in an age of nuclear weapons and highly organized guerrilla warfare and terrorism.

In the previous essay, allusion was made to the contention of the German politico-historian, Hans Delbrueck, that the Roman republic began to mutate into the empire when, in the need for greater military expertise against the Carthaginians, it was forced to introduce greater military organization and specialization into its civil life. In concrete terms, this meant less dependence on citizen-soldiers and more employment of continual or professional soldiers, on some of whom citizenship was conferred. (By the third century of the empire, Delbrueck believes that perhaps two-thirds of the Roman army was of German origin.)[1] Yet in even the highly specialized twentieth century, the United States has managed to retain the republican ideal of the citizen-soldier through use of wartime conscription, and university reserve officer training programs to supply the vast majority of officers who congeal around a relatively small core of military academy graduates. In combination with the natural advantages of this vast land, and the practical and technological talents of its people, this republican approach to providing for the common defense has been thus far successful, at least until the advent of the crisis management paradigm.

That armies of part-time soldiers have been capable at times of preserving the physical security and political freedom of their peoples against more professional armies and military societies reflects light upon the nature of the defensive use of armed force itself. The nineteenth-century, Prussian theorist of war, Carl von Clausewitz, observes in his famous book, On War, that defense is the stronger form of military action.[2] He then goes on to explain that this is evident because defense is the posture usually adopted by the weaker side, which relies upon natural advantages, familiarity with terrain, local support, and fortification to augment its military skill against an exposed invading force. It seems to have been the natural strength of the defense, in combination with some genuine military preparation and tactical skill, that has provided the "slack" (in resources and energies) for moderate political life to be achieved and to endure, by releasing citizens from the constant requirement to be soldiers. And we know that the inventiveness of peoples within the latitude to pursue other political activities and their private passions, generates arts, sciences, and technologies that often provide new strengths in war.

As a general observation, then, the rather rare achievement of republican freedom appears in historic instances of the intersection of intelligent and industrious endeavor in the spatial and temporal release provided from constant military activity to defend against external threat, with the insight and preparation to retain over time sufficient military skill to be capable of defense against external threat, or internal threat externally manipulated. If we specify our definition of political moderation to include the older instances of republican balance through mixtures of social classes, the number of cases we can cite of such historic "intersections" is not many—some of the fifth- and fourth-century B.C. Greek city-states, the Roman republic, the Swiss republic, Britain after the seventeenth century, the United States of America and some of its allies who survive as moderate regimes under the aegis of its defensive capabilities, to mention the majority.

Still, the military component of this republican balance is a relatively fragile one, both in the personalities of citizens and in the practical realm of military skill, organization, and hardware. The most dangerous times for this balance occur when militarily organized societies also come into possession of advanced hardware and strategic and tactical innovations. The military successes of Napoleon Bonaparte for a dozen years, until all of aristocratic Europe united against him, were owing to daring and aggressive artillery and infantry tactics, in combination with political successes that mobilized and brought into war the entire

French nation (some of whom in an elite, praetorian guard, Napoleon's shock troops). Somewhat ironically, it seems to have been the broad intent of the *Prussian* theorist von Clausewitz to distill from his study of the Napoleonic wars a body of military knowledge that would permit skillful defense against Napoleonic-like, "democratized" armies, without the revolutionary mobilization and militarization of entire societies.[3] Usually, it seems, militarized societies are not sufficiently innovative to be huge military threats to other countries, but occasionally a military leader is able to tap into and release in his people a channel of vital energy, and when this occurs in already developed societies, like France under Napoleon or Germany under Hitler, the result is a serious threat to less militarized societies. (Of course, even technologically less advanced countries can acquire advanced weapons technology in today's world.)

The military use of force to defend, then, provides the physical security and freedom for a people to live their own concrete way of life, by *preventing* through victory, or physical and psychological control, an enemy from occupying or controlling their territory, and asserting a new system of authority. It is distinguished from the punitive or police use of force (although in practice armies have also used force punitively) in its ability to *prevent* or control an invasion of its territory and liberty, and to maintain an autonomous system of political authority (i.e., sovereignty). By contrast, civil and police use of armed force or its deterrent threat is employed to punish, or retaliate against, disturbers of the civil order and presumed lawbreakers. Thus, the civil use of armed force to aid in preserving internal order is primarily retaliatory (after the fact) and deterrent.

This is so for two fundamental reasons. First, it is circumstantially difficult to use force to defend against disturbers of civil peace in advance of their active transgressions, if civil liberty is to be preserved. (Thus the problem of containing terrorism and guerrilla warfare among vulnerable civilian populations in non-authoritarian societies.) Secondly, since disturbers of the civil peace are usually of sufficient minority in numbers and arms that the civil police have an effective monopoly on the means of armed force, they are able to maintain order even with punitive retaliation after the fact or its deterrent threat before the fact. Anytime that opposition to civil police becomes sufficiently organized that there really are two armies at war, we recognize this in our common speech by calling the situation a civil war. Also, in such situations, armed force starts to be used militarily to defend and defeat (rather than punitively or deterrently exclusively), as evidenced, for example, in the *tactics* of urban, counterterror police forces.

The physical difference between the two uses of force arises in what Clausewitz calls the *reciprocal* nature of the military use of armed force. Because military activity occurs in the hostile interactions of independent and relatively equal opposing forces (otherwise, one side simply overwhelms the other in a large "police" action), a large amount of uncertainty and complexity arises in the independent actions and reactions of each side to actions and potential reactions of the other. As Clausewitz notes, the military arts of strategy and tactics arise in attempts to control this potential chaos through assertion of order and authority in political manipulations of the successes of skillful, battlefield fire and maneuver aimed at eventual elimination of the will and/or ability of enemy forces to continue hostilities. The military use of armed force is thus a much more complex and developed art than the police use of armed force to punish or simply overwhelm lawbreakers. This complexity arises in turn in the relative equality of opposing military forces to react independently, which capability in turn is grounded in (and supported by) the existence and energies of independent and opposing political systems.[4] (Historically, the achievement of republican freedom in the Greek city-states and the Roman republic seems to have been coeval with the development of infantry tactics that permitted successful defense against more aristocratic forms of warfare, e.g., the cavalry attack.)[5]

Now, the advent of airborne nuclear weapons, it is asserted, has relegated this view of defense to the dustbin of history because with them civilian populations can be destroyed prior to the defeat of their defending military forces. In other words, since nuclear weapons cannot be feasibly defended against on the view of the crisis management model, another basis for national security must be found. As I have tried to show, this basis was to be deterrence *of all levels* of military activity through magnified vulnerability in the face of the dangers of accidental escalation, concealed in a public doctrine of magnified vulnerability in the face of punitive retaliation after the fact. Extended to the level of conventional forces in Vietnam, this meant as well the attempted conversion of American *military* forces into quasi-military or police forces that, rather than use tactical skills to control the enemy, would locate enemy forces in order that overwhelming punitive air and ground firepower could be brought to bear upon them. Yet, as events in Vietnam corroborated, not only is such use of "military" forces very expensive and also, socially divisive, but in the absence of the intent and resolve to use firepower sustainedly and cumulatively, it is militarily ineffective even as a form of attrition warfare.

The claim, then, of the crisis management model of security that in the nuclear age provision of the common defense is no longer a feasible governing aim, and thus the purpose of military forces can no longer be to win wars, is repudiated at all levels, except the actual conduct of total nuclear war, and that can be deterred on a sounder basis than magnified vulnerability. To begin with, as the Vietnam war made clear, the threat of enlarged or escalated conflict simply does not *deter,* and certainly does not *compel,* committed revolutionary movements operating at either guerrilla or main force levels. Nor can it even keep down the casualties of one's own forces inflicted by an aggressive enemy willing to accept casualties himself, as General Westmoreland knew when he began preemptive "search and destroy" operations to hold down his own casualties, and as General Abrams knew when he sponsored the Cambodian invasion to gain sufficient slack for an orderly U.S. troop withdrawal from South Vietnam. Armies, in brief, cannot survive against an aggressive enemy without *defending* themselves—that is, taking active measures to control enemy abilities to inflict casualties and destruction—and this remains true even in the nuclear age. U.S. forces were able to evade this fundamental truth for a while in Vietnam by bringing massive and expensive amounts of resources and conventional firepower to bear upon a less technologically advanced enemy, but this would probably not be possible again for a variety of reasons. By beginning, under the rule of the crisis management model, the mutation of U.S. military forces into police forces inflicting punitive damage, rather than tactical forces using maneuver and the shock and destructive effects of firepower to defend themselves by actively controlling the enemy, we have put ourselves and our allies in a position in the NATO area, for example, where even the deterrent effect of our armed forces must rely upon the threat of uncontrollable escalation into use of nuclear weapons.

Nor does it appear that political systems can endure without attempting to provide for the common defense of the body politic. The unbalanced growth of pacifism and unilateralism, waning citizen interest in the quality of our armed forces, the successes of organized terrorism, and the doubts of our European allies about our ability and resolve to protect them have all arguably followed from our policies of magnified vulnerability under the crisis management model. If deterrence is to endure, might it not appropriately be based upon the traditional political requirement to provide for the common defense? In addition to providing a realm of political and military initiative within which to galvanize our body politic, it might also generate a more stable balance of power vis-à-vis the Soviet Union, comfort our allies, and diminish the hopes of insurgent terrorists.

What changes would be required to begin transition from a "technological" policy of deterrence through magnified vulnerability to a political policy of deterrence based at least in part upon the attempt to provide for the common defense? In terms of moderation and feasibility, the best approach might entail retention of half of the deterrent basis of the crisis management model—an ambiguous counterforce capability to make credible the deterring threat of accidental, that is, preemptive escalation— combined with a public admission and recognition of our reliance upon this deterrent threat all along; some active measures to limit damage to ourselves if nuclear deterrence should threaten to fail or genuine accidents occur; and measures to make our conventional armed forces capable of achievement of genuine military aims rather than simply punitive infliction of firepower.[6]

These measures would eliminate the contradictory aspect of the crisis management model—that is, increasing our own vulnerability while invoking the dangers of accidental war to deter the more vulnerable opponent, increasingly ourselves. They would involve the majority of the American public in a serious discussion of the basis for viable deterrence grounded in political stability. They would help lay to rest the myth of punitive retaliation as a basis for deterrence, and its naive call for "minimum deterrence." They would permit arms negotiations to be used to *limit* the kinds and numbers of weapons being produced, rather than serve to mask to ourselves the contradictory mechanism in our own model of deterrence. They would permit avoidance of the kind of arms race that might follow from attempted achievement of *unambiguous* counterforce capabilities. They would help to revitalize the American armed forces by again assigning to them a genuine military mission. They would dispel the myth that the threat of enlarged conflict can "compel" enemy ground forces to perform specific actions. And they would serve to reassure both our allies and our major adversary, the Soviet

Union, of our consistency of purpose by bringing into coincidence our publicly articulated policy aims with our real policies.

Nor need such a policy involve us in a divisive public discussion over whether there is *complete* defense against nuclear attack. The problem is to *deter* nuclear war until the century(?) of nuclear weapons is past, while maintaining political freedom and stability in this country and its allies both for its own sake and as the basis for continued deterrence. The new policy would still ground deterrence of general war in the dangers of accidental escalation, while relegitimizing the political requirement to decrease our vulnerability in the event deterrence threatened to fail, and attempting to *control* if necessary (rather than simply "deter" or "compel") conventional and guerrilla[7] enemy armed forces through application of tactical skill and the shock effects of firepower, even in conflicts with limited aims. The actual defensive measures taken to protect our people and homeland would best be a consequence of political decisions reflecting trade-offs among prudential, military, technological, and economic considerations.

Such a policy would also help to avoid the political and operational dangers of using models and vocabularies of punitive retaliation in external relations with other states. I have tried to show thus far that owing to its retaliatory (i.e., "after the fact") nature, the punitive use and deterrent threat of armed force requires massive superiority to be effective in keeping peace. It does not skillfully control a relatively equal force through fire and maneuver in the military fashion, but either disuades potential disturbers of the peace through threat of fairly certain, subsequent punishment, or it overwhelms actual disturbers of the peace by using its virtual monopoly of armed force. For this reason, it has, until the collective security ideas of the age of modern weapons, evolved largely as the appropriate method of maintenance of civil, or internal, order. To preserve the liberties of citizens, it must generally act after the fact, but with sufficient monopoly of the means of armed force to be effective (in combination with its perceived legitimacy) in keeping the civil peace. And, perhaps more important, the police use of force is correctly seen as resting for support upon capabilities for the military use of force (by, e.g., the military services and militia) to defend it against foreign invaders, or large-scale internal insurrection. In brief, it seems to be in the nature of things, even in the age of modern weapons, that the punitive use and threat of armed force is incapable of maintaining order among relative equals, and can be effective only where there is massive superiority of the means of armed force concentrated in one political authority.

The legal and political implications of treating *all* use of armed force internationally as punitive and retaliatory, as the crisis management model does, are to deny automatically the legitimacy of the use of armed force by an opposing political order; to place one's own forces in the legal and moral stance of a police power; to deny either the need for or legitimacy of attempting one's own defense through use of armed force; and to legitimize the concentration of the means of armed force by world security forces (e.g., "UN peacekeeping forces") in order that force may be used in an overwhelming and punitive fashion. In addition to denying formally the sovereignty of one's opponents, the approach dubiously implies that their political independence can be perpetuated without the provision of their own common defense. (In this sense the crisis management model goes beyond even the UN charter, which still formally permits the defensive use of armed force against military invasion.)[8] In combination with the ideological claims by the Soviet Union and others to the sole legitimate use of armed force in realization of worldwide socialist (or other) "Truth," the outcome is worldwide repudiation of the republican ideal of political independence grounded in the *defensive* (not retaliatory) use of armed force.

These developments have been afoot, of course, since at least the Wilsonian reaction to the vast destruction of World War I. They have gained momentum through the increasing destructiveness of modern and nuclear weapons, which on the one hand make it seem more vital than ever that at least world war not again occur and, on the other, seem to promise a sufficient, technological monopoly of the means of violence to allow armed force to be used effectively in a punitive rather than defensive fashion. Yet, this latter promise has been belied by several developments that together suggest that the best hope of preventing world war continues to reside in the capabilities and perceived legitimacy of sovereign states to use armed force defensively in preservation of their political independence. The first, as I have tried to show, is that the real basis of nuclear deterrence for the past two decades has not been the threat of punitive retaliation, but the credible threat of accidental, preemptive escalation (an at least quasi-defensive posture not occurring "after the fact"). The second is that since the vast monopolies of the means of violence required to make punitive retaliation effective have not been realized in the promises and threats of weapons technology (neither for the U.S. in Vietnam nor for the Soviet Union in Afghanistan), the defensive use of force has remained essential for the protection of armies. The third is that the aversion by Western governments to admit to themselves that the legitimacy of their authority is in part grounded upon police power in turn grounded upon defensive capabilities is generating the unstable cracks in their national sovereignty being filled by terrorists, revolutionaries, and pacifist extremists. And this trend threatens to accelerate as governmental authority continues to deteriorate in the failures to protect citizens.

It is this third development that presents one of the thorniest problems to be dealt with if the general political requirement to provide for the common defense is to be relegitimized in the age of nuclear deterrence. In its most virulent form this development appears as Leninist or Maoist revolutionary warfare, using the camouflage of civilian populations to protect and support incipient revolutionary forces until they are strong, while coercing, terrorizing, and coopting larger numbers of civilians into political and military participation in the revolutionary movement. While guerrilla-style "war in the shadows" is nothing new in the world, the self-imposed constrictions of our crisis management model of nuclear deterrence have permitted the Soviet Union and its allies to fashion it into a very survivable art for export. As the new art evolved in the Vietnam war, if relied upon the natural difficulties of identifying belligerents among civilian population and the constraints in the crisis management model on military use of force (e.g., not isolating the battle area) to give guerrilla warfare a sustainability it has never had, by integrating it into a comprehensive and covert war effort externally supplied and supported.

Unlike the Maoist strategy of the Chinese revolution, which moved in stages of strength from low-level covert activity to guerrilla and then main-force, conventional warfare, communist conduct of the war in South Vietnam relied after the early 1960s (but before serious U.S. intervention) upon all three stages simultaneously. Under direction by communist cadres of both North and South Vietnamese origin, local militias in villages were supported by guerrilla units around and in villages, in turn supported by main force North Vietnamese unites in South Vietnam, all levels supplied externally by the Soviet Union (and China) via North Vietnam, Cambodia, and Laos, countries also providing places of physical sanctuary for main force and guerrilla units. Thus, while maintaining strict public denial of the presence of its forces in South Vietnam, the North Vietnamese with the support of southern communists (and foreign powers) were able to establish a tight and integrated system of political and military control in South Vietnam.[9] Part of their success, of course, was owing to the willingness of American crisis managers to identify publicly the guerrilla forces as the main enemy in order to limit expansion of the war.

The advantages in this connection of rejecting the crisis management model and returning to the policy of providing for the defense of ourselves and our allies would be several and overlapping. By militarily supporting a sovereign ally under internal attack externally supplied, we would find clear and feasible tactical objectives without dissolving the authority of the local government and placing its conduct of the counterinsurgent effort at the mercy of academic models of deterrence and "compellence," and the whims of the American mass media. By demonstrating the willingness to isolate the battle area (as the British did in the Falklands war, for example) and tactically defeat any foreign, main force units present, we would also demonstrate to the world that we no longer were operating on the myth of uncontrollable automatic escalation from local military action into nuclear war. And by demonstrating that effective military use of armed force was indeed possible by the United States even in the nuclear age, we might also give less hope to future terrorists and revolutionaries, and less ground for public argument to pacifist extremists. In addition, by following this policy while making clear to our own people and our European allies that North America and Europe were two exceptional areas that we would continue to protect by deterrence based upon the dangers of preemptive escalation into nuclear war, we might gain sufficient internal support to stabilize nuclear deterrence for other generations.

1983

## Notes

1. For a detailed discussion of the "Germanic transformation" of the Roman army, see Hans Delbrück, *History of the Art of War Within the Framework of Political History*, trans. Walter Renfroe, Jr. (Westport, Conn.: Greenwood Press, 1980), vol. 2 ("The Germans").
2. Carl von Clausewitz, *On War*, book 6.
3. Ibid.

4. On the hierarchic relationship of political authority and armed force historically: "The political objective is possession as a basis for administering justice, for supporting the assertions and demands of political authority. The political requirement for sovereign authority is to enforce the law and administer an area; if there is no armed resistance to asserted political authority, simple police power is adequate to secure the rights of individuals and maintain order; if there is local resistance, the people themselves may be organized to provide back-up to the police, home guards, etc. (Blackstone: "the hue and cry"); if there is more general disorder and limited organized resistance, the people as militia may be organized into maneuver units capable of overcoming the resistance and policing the area (common in the American Revolution—in many instances militia supporting the British and supporting the Colonials fought each other over extended periods of time under officers of relatively senior rank); and if the threat to public and political order takes the form of resistance by regular forces (main force units), they together with organized militia and reserves must be overcome and disarmed if the area in question is to be politically administered." Major-General (Ret.) Wendell J. Coats, Sr., in private correspondence to the author, 4 July 1983.

5. On the relationship between military organization and constitutional development in antiquity, see Delbrück, *The Art of War*; Aristotle, *Politics*, bk. 6, chap. 7; and *The Cambridge Ancient History*, 3: 695–96.

6. See Dave Palmer, *Summons of the Trumpet: U.S.-Vietnam in Perspective* (Novato, Cal.: Presidion Press, 1978), 140–46.

7. There now appears some danger of a pendulum swing (in reaction to the Vietnam war) on the part of the U.S. military leadership away from any kind of antiguerrilla operations. See the account of departing army chief of staff General Meyer's remarks by Edward Mossberg, in "The Army Resists a Salvadoran Vietnam," *The Wall Street Journal*, 24 June 1983, p. 16.

8. Article 51, *Charter of the United Nations*.

9. For a detailed account of the relationship between Viet Cong guerrilla forces and North Vietnamese main force units in South Vietnam, see Harry Summers, Jr., *On Strategy: A Critical Analysis of the Vietnam War* (Novato, Cal.: Presidio Press, 1982).

# 9

# The Democratic Self against Moral Individualism

The Soul has Bandaged moments—
When too appalled to stir—
She feels some ghastly Fright come up
And stop to look at her—
      —Emily Dickinson, *Complete Poems*, No. 512

An important issue is being worked out in American society and politics without full awareness of its occurrence. The question is whether there are *important* parts of our individual selves that are not shared with, or communicable to, others—whether the individualist answer in the affirmative shall continue to be preserved and nurtured as a moral ideal or whether all psychic and interior experience will simply become more collective as public life becomes more interdependent.

The privacy of the individual self is like virginity in the sense that once it is lost, it is hard to remember what it was like. Yet unlike virginity not everyone starts with it, and even when it is lost or encroached upon, the occurrence may not be readily apparent. Here, the political theorist may have a proper function to perform by helping to crystallize the results of an elusive but cumulative development in our society.

In this essay, I propose to identify what I take to be the central, long-range political issue of our times—the status and future of what has been called "moral individualism." My brief account is divided into three parts: first, an identification of what is meant by "moral individualism;" next, a discussion of the views of two of its most hostile and influential critics, Karl Marx and John Dewey, but especially the latter whose influence in the United States is both more pervasive and less widely understood; and, finally, an attempt to show the centrality of this issue and the light it sheds on contemporary intellectual debate about the extension of both democracy and "rationality" into our private lives and private thoughts.

## Moral Individualism

As a moral ideal and practice, this expression is used to describe a view of life in which individuals are held to be sovereign over themselves and, as adults, responsible to others for their own conduct and choices. By "sovereign over themselves" I mean that individuals are seen in this ideal as caretakers of a fairly consistent and abiding "self," known ultimately only to themselves and, in some versions, to God. Relations with others, whether communal or intimate, are viewed primarily as external matters, since the "self" itself is an identity constituted in private, and incapable of being shared except in external action and utterance. And what makes up a "self" in the eyes of other "selves" is recognizable consistency (not predictability) in action and utterance.

Although this moral ideal had some of its implicit origins in the interior retreat from "exteriority" of Platonism and Stoicism, and although it began to crystallize in the debates of Renaissance and Reformation Christendom, this ideal, as formulated here in secular terms, would find modern adherents numbering among those who profess themselves both unphilosophic and irreligious but who have a strong sense (for whatever diverse reasons) of individual identity and distinctness. The essential thing in deciding whether one adheres to this ideal and practice comes down to the meaning of the "self" in relation to others. Upon reflection, is the "self" seen as an abiding entity, constituted primarily in private, and revealed to others only in external actions and utterances for which one is responsible? Among more modern writers, one could find, more or less, this view of things among those as diverse as Michel de Montaigne, Thomas Hobbes, and Jane Austen.

Another way of trying to get in the meaning of moral individualism is to say what it is not. This moral ideal is not to be equated with some sort of egotistic or narcissistic preoccupation with oneself to the exclusion of others. On the contrary, because relations with others are seen as external matters, these must be more attentively cultivated and nurtured than in more communal moral practices. In moral traditions and arrangements where identity is not individual, but literally constituted as part of the group, personal selfishness and "infighting" may be more at home since they pose no serious threat to the collective identity.[1] Where there is little question of an identity separate from the group, there need be little shame or forbearance at trying to dominate (or better one's position in) the group or community. The crime in collective moralities is to present oneself as psychologically sovereign without the others, or even to show unconscious signs of such a capacity.

Moral individualism is also not to be equated with the retreat into the private pleasures of "home and hearth," which Tocqueville named "individualism" in *Democracy in America*, and which he saw as a danger to public-spiritedness and political liberty.[2] (On the contrary, given his emphasis on "free choice," Tocqueville would appear to be within a tradition of moral individualism.) Moral individualism is no enemy to participation in public life—it simply requires active nurturing of public participation in order that public associations be kept vital. Where the "self" does not strongly require the group to define itself and give it identity, obligations to the group or community must be more positively emphasized.

Nor is this moral ideal to be equated with a single idea about what constitutes the "self," for example, Will, or Intellect or innate character, or an immortal soul. It simply requires, if we take our bearings from the historic practices of secular, Western public life, the acknowledgment of a private "self" that should never (nor could ever) be fully communicated to others but that is responsible for its external manifestations toward others, both as a way of coming to know its own character, and as a commonsensical condition for its own further self-disclosures.

This self-interested requirement for responsibility toward, and communication with, other "selves" leads to a few, minimal conditions for the preservation and practice of the ideal of moral individualism. If by "moral" we mean to denote relations with other "selves," then perhaps more than any other moral ideal, this one requires consistency toward others. Where the "self" is not seen to require others (in an essential way) for its identity, care for broad consistency must be exercised in utterances and actions of self-disclosure, if others are to know one's "self" at all.

This is less important in more communal moralities where there is no strong or abiding sense of individual "self." Where identity is constituted in, and as part of, a group, instances of personal inconsistency or even deceit become less momentous in moral (not necessarily legal) terms, because actions and utterances here are not disclosing an otherwise incommunicable private "self." On the contrary, utterances and actions are seen as expressing the current emphases and priorities of the group or community, and "individual self," insofar as it is seen to exist at all, is viewed as shifting or changing its composition as the priorities of the community change. Action and utterance here are primarily a means of learning, discovering, and passing on to others what the community's latest identity has become.

In a country as large and diverse as the United States, where both individual and communal moralities exist side by side, one can observe the curious situation in which the word "integrity" has come have opposite meanings, depending on who is using it. For the individualist, integrity denotes a consistent way of meeting change and disclosing oneself to others; for the communalist (or democrat as John Dewey named him),[3] integrity denotes the willingness and flexibility to reconstitute the "self" periodically as the priorities of the community shift. As a litmus test of the influence of one or the other of these two ideals, one might look to the pedagogic status of the idea of "character," denoting a relatively settled disposition in the individual—whether it endures or disappears as a quality for families and schools to instill and nourish.

If the ideal of moral individualism does have an important need for broad consistency of *purpose*[4] in relation with others, then, perhaps more than any other morality, its public life requires a literate and articulate populace, practiced at independent judgment, at "making up their own minds." In moral practices where the identity of the individual self is not permitted to shift in a fundamental way as the problems facing public associations change, there is unavoidable requirement for individuals to be capable of articulating, in detail and even with nuance, their particular viewpoint on issues. The alternatives are either "selves" who continuously recompose themselves through an ongoing process of "social interaction," or some sort of enlightened despot who looks into the hearts and minds of his subjects and "makes things right." Where citizens cannot articulate a personal view of public issues, they have no real alternative but to turn their own "person" inside out, as it were, bear their wants, fears, desires, and anxieties to others, and let someone else, or some social process, settle their view of public things. This is a possible way of living together, but it is not what has been called moral individualism. That ideal and practice, in contrast, requires listening to the views of others and weighing them against one's own perceptions of an issue, but only as part of making a judgment, in the context of more settled dispositions (principles) in one's outlook, about what should be done or not done. Moral individualism is clearly to be distinguished from listening to the views of others and sharing one's own as part of a "social process," the outcome of which will become one's view. To those who would say that everyone is always doing the latter whether they know it or not, they might ask themselves if they may not have been missing out on something. And, if they suspect they have, if this might not be their reason for wanting to make more and more of experience "public."

Another skill requisite for the practice of moral individualism—and implied in the ability to "make up one's own mind"—is the art of making judgments, the art of recognizing particular instances of more general ideas or principles. If the self is constituted fundamentally in private, and communicated to others mostly in external actions and utterances, then in addition to an articulate populace, a tradition of moral individualism also requires (and nurtures) a populace practiced at making judgments. The need for this skill follows from the centrality of general ideas in the public life of moral individualists, the only ideas that they can usually agree upon in advance, if they are not to promise away their freedom of individual choice and action. To be joined politically and civilly in terms of general ideas such as liberty, equality, and providing for the common defense requires citizens accustomed and adept at deliberation and judgment ascertaining the contingent meanings of these general ideas in day-to-day policies.

This requirement for judgment is much less necessary in situations where individuals are joined as "role performers" in some common enterprise, with assigned tasks to perform; or where action and utterance are guided primarily through communal rituals, habits, and "interaction." In such situations only leaders and managers need be practiced at making judgments in the context of more general ideas.

I believe that this brief and obviously sympathetic account of the characteristics of moral individualism is not especially controversial. One could find agreement on the outlines of this account even in the writings of such a staunch opponent of moral individualism as John Dewey.[5] (Dewey simply asserted that it had outlived its usefulness, which was to overturn the *ancien régime*.) Having set out some of the characteristics of this moral ideal, let us turn now explictly to the ideas of two of its most influential critics and opponents, Karl Marx and John Dewey.

## Marx and Dewey

### Marx

The views of Karl Marx on "individuality" are well known and need be only briefly rehearsed to show their real emphasis. In a sweeping reduction, Marx concluded that the "real" meaning of freedom and individuality had always been essentially economic freedom—the freedom of the bourgeoisie to buy, sell, and convert money into capital-producing forms. Hence, all moral and cultural ideas of individuality were merely disguised forms of "bourgeois production" and existed only for the capital-owning classes.[6] As for some sort of transcendent retreat from life into something more real or divine, this also was named an illusion that flattered itself as something other than consciousness of a particular society's productive arrangements, which must change over time as productive and other societal arrangements changed.[7] ("Society does not consist of individuals, but expresses the sum of interrelations, the relations within which these individuals stand.")[8]

In place of the old and "exploitative" ideas of individuality, Marx proposed a new "individuality" that would apparently exist and express itself *through* the community (and entire species), thereby "overcoming" all the separations and compartments of life that defined the old individuality:

> In place of the old bourgeois society, with its classes and class antagonisms, we shall have an association, in which the free development of each is the condition for the free development of all.[9]

And, more specifically, the new "individuality," the return by man to himself of his "collective essence" as a social being, will occur under communism's putative overcoming of the division of labor:

> While in a communist society, where nobody has one exclusive sphere of activity, but each can become accomplished in any branch he wishes, society regulates the general production and thus makes it possible for me to do one thing today and another tomorrow, to hunt in the morning, fish in the afternoon, rear cattle in the evening, criticize after dinner, just as I have a mind, without ever becoming hunter, fisherman, shepard, or critic.[10]

The heart of Marx's argument, as I understand it, is that because "consciousness is from the beginning a social product," and because "society does not consist of individuals but . . .interrelations," then the path to overcoming human "estrangement" is to break off trying to achieve and preserve an abiding individual identity isolated from the movement and momentum of society as a whole. In the passage just quoted, Marx seems to be implying that the need for a private self has arisen historically because of the psychic severity of being one thing in a division of labor, but that this need would go away, if under conditions of material plenty (capitalism's good legacy), we could all simply become "amateurs"—now hunters, now fishermen, now critics, and so on. Human beings, under these conditions, would "return to themselves," and overcome their "estrangement" by overcoming the need for anything private. Under conditions of material plenty, with little requirement for necessary labor, the "psyche" would, so to speak, simply be turned inside out, shared with all, made amorphous through a wide and continuous variety of experience, and reconstituted as a "social product," this time explicitly so. And all of this described as a rise (rather than a drop) in "consciousness."[11]

If seen in this light I think that Marx's argument about the real meaning of individuality heretofore as economic freedom does not require our attention for long. Once we understand Marx's beginning and ending points—consciousness as an evolving social product—it is not necessary to take his *historical* discussions very seriously. The claim, for instance, that individuality was essentially an eighteenth- and nineteenth-century economic phenomenon cannot really be argued with when isolated from the claim that "consciousness" is, and always has been, and always will be a "social product." If one suggested that there were members of the "proletariat class" who kept a part of their psychic selves private, and were thus individuals, Marx would simply object that they were taught to do this by some organized religion, itself a product of some previous, productive arrangements. And, if one objected that there were members of the "bourgeoisie" who had no self or identity outside of the flux of buying and selling, and were thus not "moral individualists," Marx would simply say that they were evolving faster than the others toward the new social consciousness, and so on. The point is that it is the claim that *all* consciousness is a social product, and that society is an expression of interrelations *only*, that must be recognized as a virtually unexaminable starting point.

It is not necessary here to rehearse all the arguments for the materialist conception of the soul and the self. For the theme of this essay, it is sufficient to note that neither Marx nor Dewey (as we shall see) can ever do more than show that *some* consciousness is a "social product," and then appeal to us with the conclusion that this is true of *all* consciousness:

Does it require deep intuition to comprehend that man's ideas, views and conceptions, in one word, man's consciousness, *changes with every change* in the conditions of his material existence, in his social relations and in his social life? (emphasis added)[12]

Both the claim that there is an interior self that abides across all social change[13] and the claim that this is an illusion are asserted starting points not susceptible of proof. This is one of those places where both sides are in the position of saying, "either you see it or you don't." What I am seeking to emphasize here is the consequences of these respective starting points. It is the totality of the unprovable claim that there is no self or consciousness that is not the expression of evolving economic and social relationships, which has become the basis for the definition of what is the desirable state of social affairs—in Marx's version, communism, and in our own John Dewey's version, "democracy." As we shall see, both desired to move toward the same general goal: universal recognition of the self as a social product, as the impetus for the complete exteriorization, communication, and psychic enervation of the self.[14] If the private and self-interested Liberal citizen (the bourgeois) could not be taught to perform his public duties of sharing, then the "self" itself would be reconstituted as a "public" thing, by way of a new educational philosophy for "democracy."

DEWEY

The views set forth by John Dewey in *Democracy and Education* (1916) seem at first reading like commonplaces to many educators today, but that is because they fail to recognize Dewey's writings as the source of many of their own (and their own teachers') ideas.[15] In a nutshell, these reduce to the idea that life is a process that posits its own end—continuous reorganization of more and more communicated and shared experience and experiment ("education"), ad infinitum. Such a situation (not a form of government, per se), Dewey named "democracy."[16]

Dewey's starting point is essentially the same as that of Marx, the idea of the self as an evolving social product, which, to be healthy, should strive for even more shared experience or social interaction. For Dewey, "moral individualism" was an evolutionary development of the eighteenth century, useful (even as an illusion) for breaking down the social and philosophic hierarchies of aristocratic civilization, but which has now outlived its usefulness.[17] It is necessary, Dewey tells us, to give up the idea of the self as something "fixed" or "ready-made," and recognize that it is "in continuous formation" through a process of social interaction.[18] Indeed, the very idea of keeping a part of oneself private or exclusive is named by Dewey as "rotten." This idea is so important in Dewey's outlook that it calls for quotation in full:

> And the idea of perfecting an "inner" personality is a sure sign of social divisions. What is called inner is simply that which does not connect with others—which is not capable of free and full communication. What is termed spiritual culture has usually been futile, *with something rotten about it, just because it has been conceived as a thing which a man might have internally—and therefore exclusively.* What one is as a person is what one is associated with others. (emphasis added)[19]

This remarkable paragraph, in my view, is the still (or perhaps agitated) center from which flows the rest of Dewey's political and educational thought. It is, as with Marx, an asserted and unprovable starting point; and, also as with Marx, it has about it the flavor of resentment at missing out on a private realm of experience. Yet it is also the basis for the rest of Dewey's prescriptions for education and public policy. And if one cannot follow Dewey in this starting point, it may not be possible to follow him where he wished to go.

Dewey's attack upon "traditional" education, from Plato to McGuffey, is directed from this unprovable starting point: because there is no unchangeable order, either in the external world or interior experience, any view of education as imparting an abiding subject matter, or nourishing unchanging personality characteristics, is an illusion (additionally, a pernicious illusion, according to Dewey, that furthers class inequalities). The only unchanging goal is continuation of life as a process of "growth," defined as more and more shared and communicated experience between groups and individuals, regardless of content (pushpin or poetry?), as long as the content can be shared.[20] Furtherance of this aim should be the aim not only of formal education, but of government as well, which should intervene in society to remove obstacles to more and more "sharing of experience."[21] (One cannot help but wonder if anything so banal has ever been elevated to a social ideal.)

The deleterious effects, over time, of such an approach to education are not far to seek. Because the only standard by which the choice and content of methods and subject matter can be judged is whether they are instrumental to the goal of more "growth" or "interaction," all scholastic standards must deteriorate from school generation to generation. If, for example, one is looking to future "interactions," then why need to know much about the past? If one already has a simple standard for the role of government, then why know much about the political arts?[22] If the majority are not very refined, and one wishes to "share" with them, then why continue to study "elitist" refinements of grammar, syntax, and expression? If there is neither transcendent nor inner reality, then why study formalisms and rituals that sensitize to such "spiritual illusions," and dam up psychic energy that could be channeled into more "social interaction?" If there is no abiding self or character, then why study *carefully* moralists from previous ages? And so on. Only experimental science, which contributes to the possibilities for social and economic growth, fares well in Dewey's view, and he never took up the consideration that over several generations of his tutelage of education, the fundamental attitudes, skills, and discipline necessary for even applied science might begin to deteriorate.

Like Marx, Freud, and other reductionists before him, Dewey mistook a part of reality for the whole. He identified an aspect, a substratum of what occurs in education and social life—what he called "growth"—and tried to make it into an explicit standard. But by making "creative growth" itself the explicit standard to aim at in primary and secondary education, the substantial bodies of knowledge and skill necessary to make such growth meaningful rather than idiosyncratic and banal, gradually began to be lost.[23] If there is no explicit standard except more "shared experience," and if the appeal to authority of teachers is denigrated because authority is inimical to more "liberation," then why should students have to learn anything in particular? Educational process, in the end, devours its own content, in a paroxysm of resentment that anybody might be excluded. This is justified on the assertion that there is *no* important and worthwhile part of the individual self that is not constituted in interaction, continuity, and communication with other selves.

## Implications

Despite their own estimates of influence, philosophers and thinkers are probably only rarely decisive in the directions of a civilization, or a nation. At the very least, the threads of their influence are difficult to unravel from others. But in politics, and the politics of education, it is not essential to see all the sources of a development to know whether to resist or support it. One can begin to discern several developments of the past three centuries all contributing, for different reasons, to what might be called the "exteriorization of the self—or, to say this more simply, demanding that all that is on the "inside" of a person be turned "outside" toward others for observation and judgment; and implying that whatever cannot be made public be relegated to the status of an inconsequential residue of private dreams and whims. Dewey did not invent this by himself.

The independent sources of this development stem from the felt need for certainty and control over societal life in the scientific age, from the spread of the idea of equality and the concomitant resentment toward distinctions, and from the pervasiveness of materialist ways of viewing and explaining all of life. These are related in turn to the spread of democracy and modern empirical science.

Modern science, as an approach to systematic knowledge for the sake of power over nature, has always demanded certainty and control over its procedures and subject matter. Since Francis Bacon, its aim has been for data systematically accumulated (by "torturing nature") in experiments reproducible by others of moderate intelligence (wits "nearly on a level"). The private, the transitory, the intuitive, and the mysterious have had little place in its largely quantitative procedures, whose very appeal has rested in the promise of certainty and control over the secrets and forces of nature. Still, the experimental method, with its requirement for fully communicable and reproducible results, remained only one approach to knowledge, until recently. Now, as is becoming clearer each decade, the fruits (and wastes) of applied science are beginning to make plausible the claim that all human knowledge and activity conform to its controlled and communicable methods, if the race is to survive. As applied science has created problems (e.g., nuclear weapons) for which it claims to have the only solutions (e.g., economically rational decision-making procedures), its entire approach to knowledge spreads as well.

For example, the most interesting aspect of the economic game theory matrices of deterrence theory[24] is their attempt, through quantitative "payoffs," to make fully "exterior" and communicable the "rational" criteria for diplomacy and tactics in the nuclear age. Minds that could not be persuaded of something like Dewey's idea of cooperative, interdependent, public selves could be forced into this new mode out of the necessity of avoiding nuclear war. The debates, for example, between "hawks" and "doves" about whether wars are started from the clash of opposing principles and interests, or through miscalculations and accidents, reflect on the surface the deeper debate over whether there is anything so permanent and abiding in the personalities of citizens that it could not be negotiated in the interest of "maximizing payoffs for all." (Whether wars can be avoided in this fashion is, of course, a separate question.)

The point of these examples is that the widespread development of nuclear weapons (and nuclear energy sources) has more than any other applied scientific development increased the plausibility, tendency, and urgency of reconstituting the human mind along the lines of the experimental method. One of the more extreme spokesmen of modern science explicitly asserts that human beings must be conditioned beyond the illusion of inner, autonomous habits of freedom and dignity, which have outlived their usefulness.[25] The psyche, in effect, must be denied (or completely exteriorized) in order that there be immediate and predictable responses to environmental manipulation.

The growing impetus to egalitarianism also threatens moral individualism. As Alexis de Tocqueville noted that, although democracies may have a taste for liberty, they have a passion for equality, and will have it whether in freedom or in slavery. ("But for equality, their passion is ardent, insatiable, incessant, invincible.")[26] Demands for formal equality, or equality of opportunity, continue to evolve over generations into demands for more substantial equality.

As the idea grows that justice and fairness mean equality, the desire to equalize things grows among even moderate citizens. But the only things that can be equalized without ambiguity are material and bodily goods, and laws and procedures relating to their distribution. Interior qualities and talents that can not be communicated, measured, and redistributed are alternately ignored and resented because there is no institutional way to articulate, control, or weigh them. This combination of political and scientific reductionism constantly urges—by its very centrality in our lives—that the only respectable explanations are materialist ones. But all of this is simply our particular version of a more general phenomenon known to ancient writers like Plato as well: democracy, in the end, is the regime of the body, because democracy loves equality, and the body and its goods and comforts are the only thing we all really have equally, or in common.[27] This was precisely why Tocqueville urged America to retain its counterweights to the tendencies of democratic materialism—formality and religion.[28]

Much of this has been observed many times, but what has not been sufficiently recognized is the potential for new alliances called forth by the coalescence of forces working for an exclusively public, cooperative, interdependent "self." Politics does indeed make strange bedfellows, but the bedfellows occasionally change. The growth of the forces working to "exteriorize the self" (whether from resentful, benevolent, or instrumental motives) holds the potential to call forth a rather unusual alliance against it—all those, who, for diverse reasons, believe it undesirable to teach and to preach to our young Dewey's formulation (or a facsimile) of the democratic "self": in brief, anyone—NeoPlatonist, Augustinian, fundamentalist Christian, "rugged individualist," nonconformist, creative artist,[29] anticommunist, transcendental mystic—who does not believe that the essence of a person is constituted in a group, shifts identity with the group, and can be communicated in all important respects to the group.

Speaking of this as a political issue, it is important to stress again what moral individualism is, and is not. The issue is not about whether one lives in relative isolation from others—without others, how could one's own character ever reveal itself? Nor is the issue (as a basis for political alliance) whether the self is made up of Will or Intellect, or an immortal soul, or simply a "very settled disposition." Nor is the issue one of egotism *versus* selflessness, or some similar dichotomy. As a contemporary Russian writer has noted, the "communalist" is often quite self-serving—what distinguishes him from the "individualist" is that he could never doubt that his fundamental identity was constituted as a part of the commune or group.[30] And for us that is the political issue as well: Shall we continue to imply to our young by word and example in the public schools that there is *no* important part of the "self" that does not arise in group interactions and shift with them?

Politically, the controversy also involves those who have no such doctrine themselves, but for whom it seems expedient to teach self-effacement in the interest of avoiding "class warfare," major political instability, and ultimately war in the nuclear age. It involves considering the viewpoint of those fearful intellectuals who think that the best hope of preserving the deeper values of Western Liberalism is never to discuss them in public or with the uninitiated.

Recall Woodrow Wilson, who foresaw at the turn of the century that, since new waves of immigrants would not understand the deferential values of the Constitution, it would be necessary to shift discussion from the ends of our political life to questions of means.[31] Being silent about ends was the best hope for their preservation. Except for the higher courts, discussion would concern itself with means-oriented public administration, rather than the Constitution, per se. This viewpoint still sets the tone for very influential policy papers and arguments. "Value questions," whenever possible, are rendered in dispassionate, technical, and economic means-oriented terms. Peace and accommodation are to be found at the "margins," both in domestic and foreign policy, on this view. Even theorists of this persuasion attempt to avoid discussion of any but easily communicable assumptions about means, such as the amount of equality necessary to make the social contract workable. Consider, for example, John Rawls's influential book, *A Theory of Justice*, which claims to be Kantian while detaching itself from Kant's transcendental arguments about the practical self (Kant must surely be turning in his grave).[32]

All of this, from Wilson to contemporary columnists who tell us not to court instability by focusing on a few "civic differences" with Marxist-Leninists, is a serious and tenacious attempt at preserving some aspects of individualism in an increasingly egalitarian world. (I do not include Dewey in even this broad sweep.) But, if it was arguably flawed as a strategy during Wilson's time, it has become a genuine liability today, because we are fast approaching the point where there is no fixed center—except civility for its own sake—around which to debate means questions, against which to measure the shifting priorities of democracy. (Who among these self-styled guardians dares dig up the treasure to see if it is still there?) And now that the family, the last institution that might judge the trends of American democracy from outside of its public concerns, is also being drawn into the democratic process with the independence of women, where shall we find the ethical ballast for the turbulent flux of democratic life?

If every group is now to enter the public realm for its fulfillment (the churches now long politicized), then ought not Dewey's claim that moral individualism has outlived its usefulness be reexamined? Our founders' solution to the diseases of democracy was to provide for the indirect exclusion of local governments, churches, and families from national political life. But now that all are to become political in orientation, perhaps the only hope for stable centers around which the restless currents of democracy might congeal is to be found in the interior and private parts of the personalities of individual citizens, outside of the web of public, democratic "interaction." But this is not possible for most people, so long as they continue to be taught by educators and opinion-making elites that *all* the important parts of the "self" are external, communicable, and shifting.

1986

## Notes

1. See, in this connection, the fascinating discussion of individualist and collectivist personalities in Alexander Zinoviev, *The Reality of Communism*, trans. Charles Janson (New York: Schocken Books, 1984).

2. Alexis de Tocqueville, *Democracy in America*, 2,2,2.

3. See, for example, John Dewey's 1916 book, *Democracy and Education* (New York: Macmillan, 1966).

4. Not consistency of means, of course, which must often change with circumstances.

5. Dewey, *Democracy and Education*, 291–305; 346–60.

6. Karl Marx and Friedrich Engels, *Manifesto of the Communist Party*, in *The Marx-Engels Reader*, 2nd ed., ed. Robert C. Tucker (New York: W. W. Norton and Co., 1978), 483–91. All subsequent references to works of Marx, or Marx and Engels, are from the Tucker edition.

7. Karl Marx, *The German Ideology*, 155–63.

8. Karl Marx, *The Grundrisse*, 247.

9. Marx and Engels, *Communist Manifesto*, 491.

10. Marx, *The German Ideology*, 160.

11. Marx seems not to have seriously considered that as the technology (to make his version of communism feasible) became more complex, the majority of human beings working with it might become more simple-minded—unless that is the esoteric meaning of Marxian communism.

12. Marx and Engels, *Communist Manifesto*, 489.

13. See, for example, the third chapter of Arthur Schopenhauer's *On the Freedom of the Will*.

14. I hope that observation of the similarity in general aims of Marx and Dewey is not controversial. It will become immediately obvious to anyone who reads, for example, *The German Ideology* side by side with *Democracy and Education*. In addition, Dewey's debt to Marx has been observed at the poles of such vast political time and space as William Ernst Hocking's 1929 review of *The Public and Its Problems* (*Journal of Philosophy* 26, no. 12), and contemporary leftist Henry Giroux's *Education under Siege* (South Hadley, Mass.: Bergin

and Garvey, 1985). Obviously, Dewey differed from Marx on the issues of violent revolution and the centrality of economic ownership.

15. For one account of Dewey's influence, see Arthur Wirth, *John Dewey as Educator* (New York: Wiley and Sons, 1966). See also B. Keenan, *The Dewey Experiment in China* (Cambridge,: Harvard East Asian Monographs, 1977).

16. Dewey, *Democracy and Education*, 81–99.

17. Ibid., 291–305.

18. Ibid., 346–60. (Apropos of Dewey's image is the image of the United States in John Le Carre's *The Perfect Spy*: Pym, the master betrayer, can find no fixed center in America or Americans to betray.)

19. Dewey, *Democracy and Education*, 122.

20. Ibid., 41–53.

21. Ibid., 81–99.

22. On Dewey's political naïveté, see Keenan, *The Dewey Experiment in China*. On Dewey's own dissatisfaction with the way his methods of "progressive education" were being applied, see John Dewey, *Experience and Education* (New York: Collier Books, 1977). But, then, if Dewey had been more politically prudent, he could not have been so "progressive."

23. As a college professor, I see a double disservice done to students by teaching them to be "creative" in primary and secondary schools, at the expense of fundamental skills of grammar, syntax, mathematical reasoning, and historical judgment. Not only have they been cheated of skills that should have become a settled "second nature" by the time they get to college, but the attempt to go back and teach them such fundamentals in college will, in fact, inhibit their fluid, or creative, self-expression.

24. See, for example, Thomas Schelling's *The Strategy of Conflict* (New York: Oxford University Press, 1960).

25. B. F. Skinner, *Beyond Freedom and Dignity* (New York: Bantam Books, 1971).

26. Tocqueville, *Democracy in America*, 2,2,1. Tocqueville thought that the growth of equality would also lead to the growth of the desire for private pleasures, but as I have already indicated, this development is not to be equated with what is called moral individualism.

27. See, for example, the eighth book of Plato's *Republic*.

28. On the importance of formality, see Tocqueville, *Democracy in America*, 2,4,7. See also the daily columns of *Miss Manners* (Judith Martin).

29. I am hopeful that creative artists would have the fastest and most intuitive grasp of the theme of this essay. *Creative* people may draw upon the psychic energies of groups and communities, but they channel this energy through some opaque medium in their personalities that is never made public or known except through its *external* manifestations—their creations.

30. Zinoviev, *The Reality of Communism*, 138–39.

31. See, for example, Woodrow Wilson, "The Study of Administration," in *The Papers of Woodrow Wilson*, A. S. Leak, ed. (Princeton University Press, 1968) 5:359–380.

32. Consider a representative sentence: "The person's choice as a noumenal self I have assumed to be a collective one"; John Rawls, *A Theory of Justice* (Cambridge, Mass.: Belknap Press, 1971), 257. In my view, the unsatisfactoriness of Rawls's way of arguing derives from his continually taking back in one paragraph what he just gave in the previous one, for example, defending

individual choice while voiding individuality of any distinctive content. This appears to be a logical "move" that Rawls has acquired from Kant, who did something similar by viewing things from both the phenomenal realm of time and the noumenal realm outside of time. But since Rawls deals only in the realm of time, the effect is simply to contradict himself.

# 10

# Liberal Democracy and the Time Stream: The Case of M.A.D.

In this essay I try to collect some age-old wisdom about long-range political stability, and put it in a form that might interest the audience of our predominantly pragmatic and scientific culture. The idea of *time* seems a good gamble for getting the attention of readers immersed since birth in ideas of growth and progress. My theme is the simple observation that no political constitution (or ordering) can endure once all, or almost all, of its values and valuations are exclusively bound in linear time, that is, find their power in being thought "timely." This statement is true both as a deduction from the definition of a political constitution, and as a practical matter as well. I believe it has relevance for modern liberal democracies as they try to move outside of the foundations laid for them by the likes of Hobbes, Locke, Madison, and Tocqueville. I shall try to show in what sense these writers (as well as the authors of the Declaration of Independence and the Constitution) suspended republican government or liberal democracy both within and without the mainstream of time; why this makes for a most stable constitutional foundation; and how we are moving toward greater immersion in time-bound values, to our detriment in a world competition with Leninists striving and managing to keep their heads above the time stream (i.e., preserve political authority).

## Liberal Republics and Time

The very idea of a constitution or regime suggests an ordering of offices, values, and priorities. Most ancient writers saw time as the enemy of order, and the decline or corruption of any political ordering as inevitable as the passage of time. Still, theorists like Aristotle saw that constitutions could be made to last longer rather than shorter, especially if they embodied the idea of proportion ("for justice is a matter of ratios," *Politics*, book 5), as in the regime mixed of democracy, oligarchy, and artistocracy.

We like to view the passage of time as a context for improvement, and modern political theorists from the late seventeenth-century on began to perceive this possibility by implying that a sovereign people could create and recreate itself in time, without the need for explicit foundings and refoundings. This idea finds contemporary political expression in something we Americans do not have in our older constitution—the European idea of parliamentary supremacy, the idea that the *latest* acts of parliament are the supreme law of the land.[1] (We, of course, still try to make the latest laws conform to the Constitution of 1787.)

The American Constitution (and the institutions it created) was an experiment to see if popular government could be made more stable than it had ever been before. It's framers, Madison said in *Federalist No. 10*, thought that it contained "the republican solution to the republican disease," that is, a way to contain the dangers of tyrannical popular faction. As every student knows, the solution included separation of power, checks and balances, and federalism. But what is the relation of these institutions to the passage of time?

The "new political science" of the American founders is plain and simple, a piece of theoretical genius about how to generate and maintain moderate political power, whose proof is in the pudding—it worked and is still working. Its arrangements are fascinating from the standpoint of time, because they synthesize and span both ancient and modern views on time, order, freedom, and progress. The lineage of our constitution runs from Aristotle and Polybius, to Renaissance humanism, to more modern writers like Locke, Sidney, Montesquieu, and Hume. Its genius was to situate political order both within and without the linear time of historically unique events, that is to situate order both in linear time, and in the cyclical time of recurring events like the seasons of life, and the general feature of human nature.

From the ancient world it took the necessity for a founding, and a fundamental law (or constitution) not easily changed. From the modern world, and its experience with civil wars over religious principles, it took the prudent understanding that democratic desires for expression of personality and economic opportunity simply could not be profitably contained within rigid forms. (Hegel said in the *Philosophy of History* that the ancient city-state collapsed because it could not contain the experience of freedom.) Our constitution attempted to ground a realm of religious and economic freedom in something less transitory: a federal republic whose compartmentalized institutions reflected insights about the recurring aspects of human nature and ambition. Its stability derived from its mixed representation of various interests, and its provision for a realm of freedom where these various groups and personalities could express themselves, compete for influence, grow richer, grow poorer, and so on. To say this a little differently, its stability has derived from institutions of authority that were outside the mainstream of time-bound changing values, but that were not inimical to the flux of more time-bound valuations, if these stayed in their proper place. Let me try to show why this system is so stable, and why it is threatened if the entire structure of authority is pulled too far into the mainstream of time-bound valuations by the increasing forces of democratization.

## Political Authority and Time

Alexis de Tocqueville observed in *Democracy in America* that the Americans were fond of operating in their daily lives on the basis of what he named, "self-interest rightly understood."[2] By this he meant that when they made sacrifices of immediate self-interest, they justified the sacrifice on the grounds that it would still benefit them personally in the long run. "Who benefits if the whole endeavor goes under?" and so on. This was seen by Tocqueville as a means of remaining free, without the rigors of classical civic virtues of public-spiritedness, and their more explicit political and civic orientation. (Indeed, Madison's arguments in *Federalist No. 51* imply that political stability lies in the direction of avoiding issues of political principle in daily life.)

The system of "self-interest rightly understood," combined with institutions of local governance and nonmaterialist religion, might be sufficient, Tocqueville reasoned, to prevent the total retreat into the private realm of the suburban pleasures, and the corruption of civic order. And, indeed, it might still be enough, if we stay aware of what is happening to our values in the largely unselfconscious process of democratization. In my view, our values are becoming increasingly time bound and conventionally determined, in such a way that even when we preserve the Tocquevillean tension between the private and the public (i.e., the more expansive private), the outcome is not necessarily relevant to the preservation of the constitutional order. Let me try to unpack this rather compact idea.

I have suggested that the stability of our republican constitution lay in providing for a contingent and changing realm of economic and social relations, grounded on observations about the recurring aspects of human nature and ambition, as reflected in governmental institutions that were unified, but not too unified, and divided, but not too divided. In other words, the stability of our arrangements of authority derives from this correspondence with reality—with the insight that politics is the middle or moderate solution to living together, and that it subsists in the tension between the mainstream of time and its peripheries, between the historically unique and the seasonal aspects that always come round again. This duality about time is reflected as well in the thought of two well-known precursors of modern liberalism, Hobbes and Locke. In spite of their other differences, both theorists grounded the contingent in something immutable or cyclical: Locke in a system of natural rights to our person and its labor; Hobbes in a system of political science designed to recall for timid citizens the memory of the perennial terrors of the state of nature, and provide roadblocks against their various avenues of return. In different ways, I believe that Hobbes, Locke, and Madison were all trying to inject a politically stabilizing element of permanence into the outlook of evangelical Protestantism, a religion of the *word* unfolding in linear time, and moving toward the end of that time.[3] At any rate, that has certainly been one effect of their efforts, and a good reason not to jettison the ballast they provided.

Yet, the spread of nineteenth-century ideas about the historicity and relativity of all values, from Marx and Dewey onward, threatens to deafen our ears to what these earlier writers still have to say to us. (Ironically, it is the Leninist followers of Marx who are resisting the historicity of all values more explicitly than we in their tenacious assertions of the inviolability of party authority, and their recognition of "objective conditions" of military reality.)[4] As the explicit and implicit views spread through our society that there are no timeless proprietary rights; that society is made up of relationships, interrelations, and roles only; and that the threat of violent death can be effectively eliminated, more and more priorities can be defined by status and relationships based solely on perceptions of influence. All of life becomes more like the market, where the value of something is its price, and its price is what people are willing to pay to have it. Political power, at least domestically within our own little world of valuations, becomes a matter of knowing "when a value created by time will be destroyed by time."[5] To relate this idea to theme of this essay, in advanced democracy the entire constitutional order starts to be drawn into the mainstream of linear time, and to lose the tension with the less mutable things that makes it a constitutional order in the first place. The effect, as in the court where the emperor had no clothes, is the loss of objectivity, reflected in imbalances with economic and military competitors not enveloped by the bubble of our time-bound conventions.

This development is not simply a theoretical issue; it is an urgent practical matter with direct policy results, and it amounts to an illusion: the belief that *all* power is attained and maintained through the movement of values in time, rather than only *some* power. I know of no more explicit illustration of this illusion than in the crisis management–arms control models devised by the Kennedy administration intellectuals, and used to structure our nuclear forces and prosecute the Vietnam war by the McNamara defense department under President Johnson. I turn to this model to provide a detailed anatomy of the time-bound and unrealistic outlook in the area of defense.

## Mutual Assured Destruction and the Time Stream

With the acquisition by the Soviet Union of nucelar weapons, the bourgeosie of the world regained a hope they had probably not had since Cobdenite liberalism, that all the world might finally be irretrievably pulled into their economic view of life. (Marx may have talked about the primary of economics, but the bourgeosie *lives* it.) The economic game theory models of conflict resolution and deterrence constructed in the early 1960s started from the presupposition that, owing to the threat of mutual assured destruction by nuclear weapons, the Soviets would finally have to tame themselves of their revolutionary outlook, and earnestly play the bargaining game of incremental or marginal gains.[6] It was believed that there was no alternative; that the latest weapons' technology of (bourgeois) civilization had made the Soviets partners in a mutual effort to "make their best deals" around the world, rather than adversaries in a dangerous contest for global domination. And the Leninists *had* to see this, the intellectuals reasoned. Unfortunately, neither the Soviets nor the North Vietnamese did see this, as any "nonbourgeois" Americans still in touch with cyclical time or nature could have told these intellectuals. Nevertheless, the models were used to direct military policy with a blindness that is best explained by the phrase, "total time immersion." In my view, the elite academies of the Northeast corridor of the United States, still so influential in the intellectual leadership of this nation, have achieved a psychic mutation describable by no better phrase. Most of this breed seem honestly to have come to believe that *all* power is about the movement and compromise of valuations in linear time.[7] Consider in this light the models the Kennedy intellectuals devised for our national security, and the legacy of which we are still struggling with.

Modern deterrence theory (at least until the current administration) claimed to be based upon the assured threat of unacceptable retaliation. The advantage in this outlook in the age of nuclear weapons is to permit policy to be based upon economically rational calculations prior to any action being taken—in other words to permit incremental alterations in the balance of power solely on the basis of perceptions and hypothetical bargaining about these perceptions. In some ways, this approach is reminiscent of the mock battles of certain pre-Napoleonic monarchs, in which outcomes were (occasionally) decided on the basis of maneuver and position without a shot being fired. The nuclear version aimed to permit the very limited and controlled use of force, and the method of control was to force each side in a confrontation to restrain itself based upon national self-interest ("self-interest rightly understood?"). To say this differently, the new method of using arms or influence under the nuclear umbrella is supposed to contain its own automatic regulatory device, if one simple rule is followed. This is that one must never directly threaten an opponent, for that would be to rupture the bubble insulating us from cyclical time or nature, and to resort to the use of real terror based on the fear and shock of imminent death. The very introduction of a state of debilitating shock in the enemy as a prelude to an action of hostilities (a traditional military objective) is to be avoided since it is not conducive to cool calculation. Rather, the opponent must be induced to restrain himself in ways that further our, rather than his, policy aims—that is, we both "make our own best deals." Thus the measure of our own skill in coercive bargaining is our ability to structure a situation such that the opponent must either back down, or take the first action to raise the nuclear ante, and who could "rationally" do that, it is asked.

I shall try to show that this is how we really operated in the Cuban missile crisis and the Vietnam war, but first it is worth noting that this is the reason why any presidential candidate who gives reason to suspect that he still has psychic links to primordial emotions is unlikely to be chosen. There is the usually unspoken fear that he (or she) would not sufficiently understand this highly stylized minuet of hypothetical intimidation, of threats based primarily on perceptions and calculations of future pain. Such a person might actually resort to the use of real terror, such as the use of *sustained* bombing to induce shock. Could, for example, a candidate with the character traits of Harry Truman any longer be elected President of the United States? At a minimum, such traits probably would be acceptable only from an actor, or someone with self-conscious distance about the image projected.

Yet, in spite of the apparent policy benefits of this national security model, it has dangers for the real balance of power, because it will work only if both (or all) sides accept its exclusively time-bound valuations, and our Leninist opponents have insisted, except in public relations exercises, in continually rejecting the outlook. (They must reject this outlook or become like Rousseau's *l'homme bourgeois*, who confused public relations, or sales, with all of life.) Where the model appears to succeed, it is because we really had the objective military power necessary to attain our aims, not because the Leninists entered into our ghostly minuet of hypothetical steps and moves. Consider three examples in this regard: the Cuban missile crisis, the Vietnam war, and the success of nuclear deterrence heretofore.

The Cuban missile crisis was the first real opportunity for the Kennedy intellectuals to apply their new science of crisis management (then called "arms control"). The overriding operational principle was to deter or compel the opponent by situating him such that he must either back down or dare to raise the nuclear stakes. In theory, then, deterrence is to issue from one's own initiative and calculation; marginal shifts in relative influence can take place; heads stay cool; and escalation of conflict is contained. This is why the device of a naval blockade or embargo was chosen—to put the initiative back in the Soviets' hands to deter themselves. This operating principle was also why the Kennedy administration became frantic after one of our reconnaissance aircraft was shot down over Cuba, and others continued to be fired upon in spite of our warnings to desist.[8] We had to have reconnaissance, yet if another of our planes were hit, the burden of the military initiative would have been back on us to up the nuclear stakes or back down. We thus quickly worked out some sort of secret arrangements in which, apparently, the Soviets withdrew their missiles in Cuba in return for our promise to withdraw some in Italy and Turkey. But the point is that we got what we got not because of the model, but in spite of it. The nuclear "balance" in 1962 was so preponderantly in our favor, and our military advantage in this hemisphere so obvious, that we could simply have dictated terms, had we chosen.[9] Yet it was the belief that the model had worked, that the Soviets had put on the model's veils of self-consciousness (between bargaining and the resort to the real threat of death), which led to a genuine tragedy as the model was applied without alteration ten thousand miles away to circumstances in which our real power was not so preponderant that we could use it "marginally."

Almost all of the paradoxes of the Vietnam war can be explained once it is seen that our plan for the endeavor was none other than the crisis management paradigm of the Kennedy intellectuals,[10] and its attendant confusion of real power with the exclusively time-bound valuations of the *l'homme bourgeois*. Consider the reflections of the then British Consul general to Hanoi, Mr. John Colvin:

> Victory by September 1967 in American hands . . . was not so much thrown away as shunned with prim, averted eyes. . . . Even now this renunciation is difficult to understand. . . . Nor, above all, could it [a war] be won by men ashamed of America.[11]

Satisfaction is available for Mr. Colvin's puzzlements without resort to the charge that the administration intellectuals were ashamed of America, or that victory was "shunned." I believe that the McNamara defense department and its ivy league advisors were as "patriotic" as the *l'homme bourgeois* is capable of being within his linear time-bound valuations; and that they were even prepared to gain the political end of forcing the North Vietnamese out of South Vietnam, if this could be done consistently with the requirements of the crisis management model that we not take the military initiative in the conventional sense.

I shall turn to this in a moment, but here is a good place to remark how this tragic history highlights that the genius of the bourgeois, as essentially an urban creature, is his sensitivity to relative and marginal fluctuations in human relationships of influence, but that this mind-set is also the source of his blindness about real power relations constituted in the perennial events of cyclical time (e.g., the threat of violent death), and capable of puncturing the artificial compartments of his self-conscious urbanity. This insight was what led the thinkers of the eighteenth-century Scottish enlightenment to observe that commercial or bourgeois society could retain its common sense only so long as it could sustain the willingness to *defend* itself.[12] Somewhat ironically it is that bastion of capitalism, *The Wall Street Journal*, that has retained much common sense on defense issues, and refused to be drawn into the confusion between real power and power based solely on perception. Perhaps this is because its editorial outlook is so close to the pages of Adam Smith's eighteenth-century works, which still grounded economic freedom in less ephemeral aspects of human nature. Smith's visions would not yet fit Rousseau's prescient account of the *l'homme bourgeois* as the man, who, when he tries to think of others, thinks only of himself, and when he tries to think of himself, thinks only of others.[13] In the terms of this essay, Rousseau's bourgeois, or city dweller, has no fixed points; his consciousness is completely within the mainstream of time. All of this suggests that the genesis of this type has more to do with urban intellectual forces of the nineteenth and twentieth-centuries, than with eighteenth-century capitalist thought, still (partially) grounded in resistance to the industrial development of a "one-dimensional man."[14]

To return to the illusions of the time-bound, crisis management model, consider the following paradoxes of the Vietnam war: despite countless U.S. battlefield successes in the South combined with massive bombing in the North, we still were unable to attain our modest political goals in the war. Whether we could have attained them using strategies concerned with real power rather than perceived durational power is another issue.[15] At the least, such a strategy would have made us more realistic about our chances. My concern here is simply to show that our strategy really was the time-bound crisis management paradigm of the Cuban missile crisis, which attempts to use infliction of pain incrementally to influence "rational" calculations about marginal gains and losses, in order to alter relative power relations under the nuclear umbrella. Memoranda and documents from the McNamara pentagon show that this outlook directed our war effort and that, by about 1967, the political appointees in the Department of Defense had decided that the model was not working;[16] but democracy moves slowly, and it took another seven years to get out of Vietnam. The model was not only irrelevant for use against the North Vietnamese politburo who were not thinking at all in terms of a minuet of threats at the brink of nuclear escalation,[17] but it also drove our military tactics— still grounded in the Hobbesian threat of violent death—against the urbane civilian strategy of "arms and influence." The results, to say the least, were counterproductive. The major point of friction was, and is, that military strategy (although it includes perceptions) is still grounded in cyclical time and real power, and requires tactical initiative to control events on the battlefield and induce shock and disorder in the enemy; the crisis management model, by contrast, is grounded solely in perceptions of relative influence, and uses small bursts of force incrementally to induce "enlightened" bargaining. For this reason, it is not interested in inducing shock in the enemy leadership, or in taking the risks of military initiative. (I believe this is one clear case where the Western urge to synthesize disparities has run into objective limits in the nature of things.) The model is the real reason why we did not bomb consistently to induce shock in the North (except for eleven days in December 1972 to get Paris bargaining talks resumed),[18] and why we would not link together our battlefield successes to isolate the South logistically and try for conventional military victory. All of these measures would have penetrated the veil of duration-based values, and propelled us back into the presumably uncontrollable realm of cyclical time and the threats of the Hobbesian state of nature. Also, as is now well known, after the "Tet Offensive" of 1968, the American press and people simply wanted out—but up until then, the major constraints upon the administration's political and military goals were the unrealistic and inappropriate assumptions in the "new science" of arms and influence from which it operated.

Before leaving this subject, it is instructive to look at another instance where, as in the Cuban missile crisis, our models of perceived power appear to have worked, while actually relying on something outside of rational calculations about marginal gains. This is the real success of nuclear deterrence heretofore in preventing major military aggression. The theory of assured destruction says that what deters aggression is the perceived threat of unacceptable retaliation after the fact. If this is correct, than we can probably continue to live comfortably outside the Hobbesian realm of real threats of death—continue to remain within our controllable world of coercive bargaining for incremental gains under the nuclear umbrella. But, in my view, while the success of deterrence in the past three decades is indisputable—at least at the nuclear level—the perceived dangers of unacceptable retaliation have not been the real operational deterrent. Rather, and this is a terrifying thought for the *l'homme bourgeois* in his controlled urban environment, the real deterrent has more likely been the uncertainty and possibility of accidental escalation into nuclear war. The Soviets always cogently argued back to us (at least prior to the Reagan "SDI" proposal), that if our real strategy was punitive retaliation after the fact, why was it we needed so many first-strike weapons. These weapons, of course, were the concrete expression of the views of (nonbourgeois) military minds in various administrations, but they also reflect the implicit realization that what really deters is the possibility of preemptive or defensive strikes on other missiles and the uncertainty the prospect generates in the minds of the opponents.[19] The more reasoned views of the current administration in support of their "strategic defense" program reflects appreciation of this reality: "SDI," they say, is intended to *enhance* deterrence by introducing greater uncertainty in the minds of Soviet decision makers about our own abilities to defend ourselves and frustrate their initiative.[20] This administration's rhetorical arguments, at least, are moving further away from the ghostly minuet of hypothetical intimidation that characterizes the assured destruction paradigm.

I have dwelt at length on the anatomy of the assured destruction model in order to illustrate one of the dangers of the spiral into a world of exclusively time-bound valuations of our own creation. It is a dramatic and demonstrable instance of our potential for this pathology. But there are other problems that we will have to face as we are tempted, by democratic hostility to hierarchy and static order, to make all of our important criteria for allocation of opportunities and resources the artificial ones of our creations in time. The danger in the development for our own system is loss of authority to make unpopular decisions; the danger vis-à-vis external competition is loss of objectivity about our own capabilities (or lack of them). For example, in domestic politics, we will have to watch the extension of the "one man, one vote" principle now used for congressional districting purposes. If it is equitable in that sphere, it will be argued, then why not extend it to eliminate the unequal senatorial representation of smaller states, and their undemocratic influence in the electoral college? In time, the cities, with their linear-time valuations may completely eliminate the outlook of the more cyclical-time-oriented country-side, already fast diminishing on its own.

Externally, there is the danger over the structure and composition of our defense forces, if we fail to isolate objectively in our own minds the real reasons for the success (and limits) of deterrence, heretofore. This point has been discussed at some length already. But, another external problem is our relation with trading partners like the Japanese and Germans, who are already saying that the Americans are living beyond their means. What might keep us honest in that sphere is allowing world market forces their due in our monetary and tariff policies and compelling our trading partners to do the same. Systematization of economic laws of supply and demand by Adam Smith and others occurred in the eighteenth-century, a century not yet so deeply immersed in time-bound valuations as our own. Even though nominal prices are set by what buyers are willing to pay, we all know that these are objective aspects to the interplay of buyers and sellers, capable of puncturing the air-tight compartments of artificially created valuations. But, above all else, and regardless of what we decide in any one policy or law, the hope for our duration as a constitutional order lies in regaining something that our historicized urbane outlook threatens to obscure. This is the insight that our stability and longevity have derived from republican institutions expressing *both* the linear time-bound valuations of *l'homme bourgeois, and* the more abiding, cyclical time valuations of the politically minded among our citizenry. To enter the linear-time stream completely, like a bumpkin seduced by city lights, is to risk squandering our substance very quickly. The key to longevity is knowing how to use our inherited political capital without using it up.

1987

## Notes

1. See, for example, Samuel Huntington, *Political Order in Changing Societies* (New Haven: Yale University Press, 1968), 93–139.
2. Alexis de Tocqueville, *Democracy in America*, 2,2, 8.
3. For a discussion, see, for example, J. G. A. Pocock, "Time, History, and Eschatology in the Thought of Thomas Hobbes," in *Politics, Language and Time* (New York: Atheneum, 1973), 148–201.

4. For an account of authority in contemporary Leninism, see Flora Lewis, "Communism Without Marx," *New York Times Magazine*, June 1987.

5. Alberto Moravia, "The Terrorist Aesthetic," *Harpers Magazine* (June 1987): 38.

6. See, for example, Harvard economist Thomas Schelling's *The Strategy of Conflict* (New York: Oxford University Press, 1960), and *Arms and Influence* (New Haven: Yale University Press, 1966).

7. For a nonmilitary example, consider the well-known Rawlsian proposals for attaining social justice: the "veil of ignorance" and the "difference principle." Both are notional devices intended to reverse *in time* inequalities occurring before birth.

8. For an outline of events in the Cuban missile crisis, see A. George, "The Cuban Missile Crisis, 1962," in *The Limits of Coercive Diplomacy* by A. George, D. Hall, and W. Simmons (Boston: Little, Brown and Co., 1971), 86–143.

9. For a similar view, see Peter Rodman, "The Missiles of October: Twenty Years Later," *Commentary* (October 1982); 39–45.

10. See Wallace J. Thies, *When Governments Collide: Coercion and Diplomacy in the Vietnam Conflict, 1964–68* (Berkeley: University of California Press, 1980).

11. John Colvin, "Hanoi in My Time," *The Washington Quarterly* 4, no.2 (Spring 1981): 153–54.

12. See J. G. A. Pocock, "Civic Humanism and Its Role in Anglo-American Thought," in *Politics, Language and Time*, 80–103.

13. See Allan Bloom, Introduction to Rousseau's *Emile*, trans. Allan Bloom (New York: Basic Books, 1979), 4–5.

14. See Albert O. Hirshman, *The Passions and the Interests* (Princeton: Princeton University Press, 1977).

15. See Dave Palmer, *Summons of the Trumpet* (Novato, Cal.: Presidio Press, 1978), and Harry Summers, *On Strategy* (Novato, Cal.: Presidio Press, 1982).

16. See the various memoranda of the McNamara defense department collected in G. Porter, ed., *Vietnam, A History in Documents* (New York: Meridian Books, 1981).

17. See Thies, *When Governments Collide*, 111–62.

18. See Palmer, *Summons of the Trumpet*, 252–54.

19. See Wendell J. Coats, Sr., "Clausewitz's Theory of War: An Alternative View," *Comparative Strategy* 5, no. 4 (1986): esp. 367–71.

20. See, for example, Kenneth Adelman, "SDI: Setting the Record Straight," in *Promise or Peril*, ed. Z. Brzezinski (New York: Ethics and Public Policy Center, 1986), 199–205.

# Epilogue: Logic and Civility as "Will to Power"

These essays have defended the activity of politics as providing the "moderate solution to living together" and, more specifically, as providing for the moderate reconciliation of differences. The title of this epilogue names two civilized achievements that combine to make possible the moderate reconciliation of differences among people in modern liberal polities—logic and civility. Both evolved historically as ways of mediating conflict among diverse tribes and nations, and both are expressions of the personalities of particular civilizations. The first is a gift of the ancient Greek city-states, especially Athens, codified during the decline of that civilization in the works of (the non-Athenian) Aristotle, and carried to other lands by his former pupil, Alexander the Great. The second is a gift of early modern European civilization, the fruition of centuries of attempts to reconcile the richly diverse inheritances of its peoples—the laws of Moses, the Christian revelation, Greek logic, Roman law, papal authority, tribal customs, local laws and languages, and so on. In a time when both logic and civility are under heavy criticism for their "biases," it is worthwhile reminding ourselves of what they make possible for us.

Most people probably never master more than the ability to perform a simple syllogism, and even this mastery may remain largely intuitive, but that is enough for the moderate reconciliation of differences in most practical matters. To be capable of seeing, for example, that if all men are mortal, and if Socrates is a man, then he must also be mortal, is to gain access to two principles of "universal" or "public" communication. It is to see that if something is true (mortality) of the larger category (mankind) to which something else belongs (Socrates), then it is true of that particular being also (Socrates is mortal). And it is also to see, or agree, that contradictions are logically unacceptable—that Socrates cannot be both mortal and immortal in the same instant. There may still be disagreement over the initial assumptions: Are all men mortal? Is Socrates a man? Is defense spending always inflationary? But once the initial assumptions are accepted, there is public agreement on what is persuasive.

It is perhaps not always appreciated what a remarkable achievement it is when large numbers of people (e.g., the "Cartesian middle classes") are capable of grasping and applying even this amount of logical reasoning. There is provided an alternative to all sorts of appeals to emotion, authority, and threat in the first instance, to resolve differences. Nor is it a lethal criticism of logic to note that it is observed more often in the breach or that, in the end, the appeal to authority is the final political arbiter. This is simply to observe that most human beings are not so abstract as to be solely creatures of logic, but this does not take away from the greater likelihood of their acceding to authority when its conclusions are logically demonstrated as well.

It is perhaps also not sufficiently appreciated how "universal" or "public" is the language of logic. The ancient Greeks may have thought of it as exclusively their own achievement, almost like an esoteric religion. But, in fact, it is a most publicly accessible "religion," open to any people capable of performing a few simple mental operations. The lucid gift of a civilization whose language and culture were built upon "seeing" clearly with the mind's eye, logic is the antidote to the abuses of the intuitive, the mysterious, the revealed, the irrational, and the occult, and hence a most appropriate public or political language. Even the reductionist critiques of logic, from Marx, Nietzsche, and Freud to the radical feminists, all use logic to try to debunk logic. The charges are made that it is simply the revenge upon history of the ugly and resentful; that it expresses the "will to power" of the unnecessarily abstract masculine personality; that it is no more than the "false consciousness" of idle theorists who do not grasp what they owe to the collective labor of the community; that it cannot be trusted because it is always driven by the irrational. Although there may be a speck of truth in each of these extravagant claims, one cannot help but wonder if those seeking to dethrone logic as the final arbiter in both the classroom and the political forum have seriously considered the implications of its displacement by emotions and felt needs, and the vacuum created to be filled by the coercion of collective impulse, and those who can control and manipulate it. May it not, in fact, be the case that there is no more suitable public language for moderately reconciling differences among peoples of diverse backgrounds and interests than Greek logic, especially if tempered by modern European and Anglo-Saxon practices of civility?

It is civility that moderates the potential in logic to be carried to tyrannical extremes and enforced by philosophic kings. Logical conclusions, if based on an initial premise that the highest thing in the human being is the ability to reason logically, can be quite intolerant and immoderate for the less intellectually well endowed. A well-known description of a grotesque city built exclusively for the needs of the philosophic intellect can be found in Plato's *Republic*, but the lesson of that story is the unlikelihood of such a city ever coming into being, and hence, the reasonableness of pursuing philosophy in private. (See, in this connection, the last few paragraphs of book 9.) Less grotesque, but equally intolerant of the less intellectually well endowed, is the account of friendship in the latter books of the *Nichomachean Ethics* of Aristotle, which explains that true friendship is only possible among equal partners in the philosophic life. In the end, if theoretical intellect is the highest thing in the personality, then everything else must logically serve it, insofar as this is politically prudent and feasible.

Medieval Christian civilization confronted a dilemma in this regard, as Aristotle's political and ethical writings found their way back into Europe via Latin translations. How could it reconcile Aristotle's powerful and recondite account of the primacy of intellect and the virtues of political life with the teaching of their religion on the primacy of faith, hope, and charity, and the relative unimportance of earthly and political life? One well-known systematic attempt was of course, the *Summa Theologica* of Thomas of Aquino, which simply placed the "theological virtues" on top of the intellectual and practical virtues ("Gratia non tollit naturam sed perficit"), but many have protested that the Thomist solution was more Aristotle than Christ. Furthermore, with the increasing powers of local sovereigns and their various nations, the European peoples had even more pressing problems than merely theoretical differences between Christ and Aristotle.

After a period of religious wars between Catholics and Protestants, and Protestants and Protestants, when it looked as though Europe might destroy itself, the European peoples achieved an outlook, by way of the Latinized abstractions of their medieval heritage, that would never have been possible for the warring Greek city-states in their straight-forward lucidity. This outlook, over time, has come to be called "civility," and might be summarily described as the willingness to recognize and respect the formal equality of the human personality, *qua* personality, while suspending public judgment on as many of its substantial aspects as are consistent with civil order in the circumstances. This outlook arose from, and permitted, the reconciliation of the individualist premises of non-Aristotelian Christianity with the requirements of civil and political order among peoples and nations of diverse background; in time it gave a new defense of private property; it produced the separation of church and state; it produced the idea of a constitution of *general* laws interpreted by individual judgment; it produced the idea of politics as the formation of, and deliberation about, such general laws; this outlook can be found, to differing degrees, in political theories as far apart as Hobbes's *Leviathan* and the latest writings of John Rawls (who cannot clearly decide if he belongs to this tradition, and, like St. Thomas, appears to be aiming at scholastic murkiness as the road to civil peace).

Yet, I believe, it is a mistake to say that these political arrangements are ethically neutral as Rawls and others have tried to maintain; that they do not make a claim about the "good life."[1] They are no more neutral than Greek logic, and are clearly a secular Liberal version of the Protestant solution to the tension between the values of evangelical Christianity and those of pagan politics.[2] They are an expression of the "will to power" of a particular civilization with a strong disposition toward preservation of the psychic privacy and moral sovereignty of the individual personality, and their adoption closes off any number of political possibilities requiring substantial involvement of human beings in the lives of one another as a constitutional principle.

In this sense, the manners of civility resist not only the potential for tyranny in logic, but the potential for chaos in the permissiveness of extreme democracy.[3] The danger to order in extreme democracy has always been the attempt to collapse the "hypocritical" tension between the public and private things, by making public all the private bodily needs, wants, and pleasures, while eliminating the truly public things (like duty and honor) as now unnecessary. As I tried to show in a previous essay, this is the effect of the democratic ideas of John Dewey, and of the young Marx as well. But widespread practices of civility, by preserving the formal distinction between the public and private aspects of the personality, unconsciously resist the egalitarian urge in extreme democracy to turn the soul inside out, make public and communicable almost all of life, and try to live completely in terms of conventionally created, time-bound values of near total toleration and permissiveness. Yet, so long as numbers of people continue to be raised in traditions of civility, this development can be resisted—that is, the forces of democracy may be unable to extinguish completely the residues of republican citizenry.

In brief, the manners and practices of civility constitute an ethical choice about how to live, which use, but try to limit, the gifts of our ancient Greek inheritance, and are clearly prejudicial to political visions that would encroach very far on individual privacy. Yet, as these essays have suggested, they still constitute the most manageable arrangements for the toleration of diversity available to us, and those who would keep them vital require to know the conditions for their maintenance.

Finally, although it is another theme, if it is asked why preserve liberal civility and toleration of diversity, the most straightforward answer is that it is the supreme expression of the impulse of the Western personality to stand both within and without the stream of time; to take the contingent seriously, and yet to rise above it.[4] The philosophic foundations of modern liberalism, as laid by Hobbes and Locke, expressed this duality about time: they permitted a realm of time-bound changing economic relations, anchored in something immutable—the threat of violent death for the one, and inalienable, natural rights for the other. To give up the institutions that express the complex Western urge to live in both realms would be to let go of the tautness and willfulness in the personality necessary to span them both, and to imply that we too had espied the moment of our death in time,[5] and admitted our political mortality. Perhaps it is too soon for that.

1987

## Notes

1. See John Rawls, "Justice as Fairness: Political Not Metaphysical," *Philosophy and Public Affairs* 14, no. 3 (Summer 1985): 223–51.

2. See G. de Ruggiero, *The History of European Liberalism*, trans. R. G. Collingwood (Oxford: Oxford University Press, 1927).

3. For a penetrating account of such developments in contemporary America, see the first part of Allan Bloom's *The Closing of the American Mind* (New York: Simon and Schuster, 1987). Bloom's hope, however, lies not in the direction of civility, but closer to something like Socratic *eros*, understood as an obscure, and hence putatively salutary, form of atheism.

4. See, in this connection, Reinhold Niebuhr, *The Nature and Destiny of Man* (New York: Charles Scribner's Sons, 1941).

5. In my view, the political successes of President Ronald Reagan, so perplexing to the fashionably time-bound urban left, are owing in part to the popular support he has received precisely for his adamant refusal to permit the ap-

pearance of the mortality of this republic, or to concede symbolically that the destiny of the world might no longer be identical with the destiny of the United States of America. For some insightful observations on the mortality of republics, see Niccolo Machiavelli, *Discourses on the First Ten Books of Titus Livius*, introduction to book 2.

# Index